The Warriors
✶ ✚ ✚ And
The Bankers

A
History
Of The
Knights
Templar
From
1307 To
The
Present

Alan Butler
Stephen Dafoe

Templar Books
Belleville - Ontario - Canada

Templar Books
83 Purdy St.
Belleville, Ontario. Canada
K8P 1Z2
www.templarbooks.com

Copyright © 1998 by Alan Butler and Stephen Dafoe

Canadian Cataloguing in Publication Data

Butler, Alan 1951-
The warriors and the bankers: a history of the Knights
Templar from 1307 to the present

Includes bibliographical references.
ISBN 0-9683567-2-9

1. Templars. I. Dafoe, Stephen 1962- II. Title.

HS745.B88 1998   271'.7913   C98-901188-7

Printed and bound in Canada

10 9 8 7 6 5

The Warriors and the Bankers

Contents

This Book Is Dedicated To:

Christopher Knight and Robert Lomas

"Who set so many balls rolling"

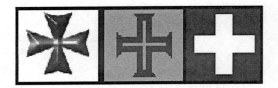

Introduction

"Oh What A Web We Weave"

A year or two ago a book such as this would have been something of an oddity. For although, as with other books of its nature, two authors have pooled their research and talents to create what you are about to read, most of our cooperation took place via the Internet. Alan Butler lives in Yorkshire, England while Stephen Dafoe lives thousands of miles and a couple of time zones away in Ontario, Canada. We two authors came together thanks to Stephen's Templar Web site, and it is also because of the World Wide Web, that we decided to put our combined knowledge and research resources together to write this book.

In fact this is all rather providential, because it is towards another sort of World Wide Web that we now cast our gaze, but this one is of a much earlier date and refers to the web spun by the still mysterious, though nevertheless extremely successful Knights Templar who rose from humble beginnings in 1118 to become a force of power and influence throughout the whole known world of their day, until their destruction in 1307. We decided to write what follows, as a direct response to the questions we are both regularly asked concerning the fate of the Knights Templar after 1307.

In the pages of this book you will find many theories as to the fate of the Templar knights after the persecution meted out to them by the Crowned Heads of Europe and the Pope in and after 1307. Some readers may be familiar with certain of the suggestions that follow, whilst others represent our own collective theories, based on the latest research into this age-old mystery. In particular we would wish to draw the reader's attention to the chapter concerning Switzerland, which although not previously suggested as a resort for post 1307 Templars, has presented us with such convincing evidence, that we remain convinced that the Templars not only survived, but that they created a 'State' or their own in the Alps.

The Poor Knights of Christ and the Temple of Solomon, as the Templars were more properly known, were responsive to one primary location -Jerusalem. To the medieval cartographer,

Jerusalem was drawn as the 'navel' or center of the known world. It is from this epicenter that knowledge, spirituality and culture spread throughout the known and unknown world. The importance to the world of the Holy City has not diminished to this day and Jerusalem retains its place as a 'sacred site' to Christian, Muslim and Jew alike.

Like the Holy city and its most famous Temple for which they were named, the Knights Templar too spun their own silken threads of knowledge, protection and influence throughout the known world. On the way they created a network of communication and commerce that would take them from the Levant to every corner of Europe, parts of Asia, Africa and, almost certainly, to the Americas. It is this enduring web of influence and power that we wish to address in this book.

Every quest must have its point of departure, and for ours we would like to use the words of a fourteenth century poet who asked the following question:

"The Brethren, the Masters of the Temple,
Who were well-stocked and ample
With gold and silver and riches,
Where are they? How have they done?
They had such power once that none
Dared take from them, none was so bold;
Forever they bought and never sold...."

It is to this unknown poet and you our reader, that we will try to answer that so often asked question; "What became of the Knights Templar?"

Alan Butler
Stephen Dafoe

September, 1998

Chapter One

Up To Their Fall

As the sun began its rise on the morning of Friday the 13th of October, 1307, a series of raids occurred simultaneously throughout all of France. Troops, perhaps loyal to, but certainly in the employ of, the king of France, swept in at dawn to arrest members of the monastic order known as the Knights Templar. The reasons for these arrests were a series of accusations against the monastic order that ranged from idolatry and demon worship to spitting on the Holy Cross. These charges, although not the topic of this work are mentioned only to place later events in their historical context. Stephen's previous research had shown strong evidence that these charges were false and invented by the King of France, Philip IV, as a means to procure the vast Templar fortune, much of which is believed to have escaped his clutches. What became of this wealth and the noble order, which had amassed it, is the topic of this book and will be examined in due course.

Before any such discussion can commence, we feel it is important, for you the reader, to be offered a brief understanding of the events that led up to those arrests. In order to do this, we will need to back our story up two centuries to the year 1099 and the victory of the First Crusade. On July 15th of that year, the Crusaders had managed to capture, or in the eyes of the Christians, rescue, the city of Jerusalem from the Seljuk Turks, who had previously occupied the city. This crusade, known today as, the First Crusade, began four years earlier, in Claremont, France, when Pope Urban II gave a moving speech, that would bring many men to put down their tools and pick up the sword. After a rough false start, known as the Peoples Crusade, the Crusaders persevered and obtained the aforementioned victory on July 15th in the year 1099.

The Holy Lands, now in Christian hands, offered the possibility for pilgrims to travel from Europe to view the land where their Lord, Jesus Christ, had walked and taught. But although the routes were open for Christian travelers to pay homage, the actual roads were dangerous and often deadly places. Many pilgrims were robbed, raped and even murdered on route.

At this stage in history along came Hughes de Payens a French knight and hero of the First Crusade. De Payens, realizing the danger to the lives of his fellow Christians offered his service and that of eight of his companions to act as protectors and police along the roads to the city of Jerusalem. His offer was welcomed with open arms by King Baldwin of Jerusalem, brother of Godfroi de Bouillon. De Bouillon, one of the leaders of the First Crusade was offered the crown of King of Jerusalem, but refused the title on the basis that he didn't see it fit to be named King in a land where the real King, Jesus had lived. His brother, Baldwin saw no problem in assuming the mantle and later became the first European King of Jerusalem. Being appreciative of De Payens offer, Baldwin II granted Hughes and his men the area on the Temple Mount, occupied by the Al Aqusa Mosque, which legend goes occupied the very same spot as the Temple of Solomon. It is from this base of operations that the order derived the name, "The Poor Knights of Christ and the Temple of Solomon" or as they later came to be known, the Templars.

St. Bernard
of Clairvaux

The poor allusion in the orders name came from its self imposed vow of poverty, by which no member was to have any personal property. All possessions of the order belonged to the institution as a whole. Impoverished at their inception, the Templars may have been, but poor they would not remain for soon the order attracted the favor of noble and monarch alike. Many of these Lords and heads of state gave gifts of money and land to the fledgling order, so much so that the order soon began to lend it to others. This money lending occurred at a time when usury was forbidden by the Church.

It is likely that the reader will question how a diffuse group of medieval guardian angels, could become so popular in such a short time as to receive the ears and pocket books of the nobility. The answer is quite simple, they did so with some high ranking assistance. This help came in the form of the Cistercian Abbot, Bernard of Clairvaux, later to be canonized as Saint Bernard. Bernard, a man often referred to as the Second Pope, was without a doubt, the principle spokesman for Christianity in his day and with his high and lofty status, knew that what he said and felt would be not only listened to but generally accepted as Gospel. It was Bernard's letter to his friend Hughes de Payens entitled, "In Praise of the New Knighthood", that not only endorsed the Templar order, but elevated it above the rival and older order, the Hospitallers.

Bernard's letter praised the Templars for their piety and selflessness in their cause, while at the same time damning the secular knight as self centered mercenaries bent on a single-minded cause of obtaining the spoils of war. It was this letter that would popularize the order in the eyes of the nobility.

In 1127, Bernard continued his support for the order, by assisting the council of Troyes, in creating the Templar's Rule of Order, which he modeled after his own Cistercian Rule of conduct. Along with this new rule came the concept that the Templars need answer to, nor be accountable to none other than the Pope. Perhaps it was this autonomy, combined with the already growing wealth that allowed the order to expand at such a rapid rate. As history would show it certainly would be the combination that would lead to their ultimate downfall. Without going into a complete history of the years between the formation and subsequent downfall of the Templars, of which we have no doubt many readers are already aware, suffice it to say that the order grew to become the most feared and respected of the monastic fighting orders. Many accounts have been written by historian and journalist alike, about the Templars skills in warfare, seamanship, commercial acumen and even banking. So completely accepted was this order that it must be asked, where did the Templars go wrong along the way, allowing the chain of events that followed to be forged, link by link, leading to their eventual arrest?

In 1187 after nearly a century of Christian occupation, the Holy Land, fell back into Muslim hands. This time those hands belonged to the Saracen leader, Saladin. Much has been written of the battle of Hattin in which many Crusaders and Templars lost their lives. On that fateful day, the Crusaders had fought long and hard, but to no avail. Saladin's men were equally well trained warriors and outnumbered the crusaders by a large margin. The Christian army was surrounded and its men captured. So feared by Saladin were the Templars, that while the Crusading knights were being bound together as slaves, the Templars were forced to their knees and instantly beheaded. There are accounts of the Crusaders running forward claiming to be Templars, preferring a quick merciful death to the life of an infidel's slave.

After the loss at Hattin and the later fall of Acre one century later in 1291, there is no doubt in our minds that the Templars lost favor in the minds and hearts of the European peoples. Certainly as the leading monastic warriors they represented, the Templars were held to blame for the loss of the Holy Lands. So the Templars, with no more wars to wage, returned to their preceptories, castles and churches, scattered throughout Europe, to engage in what they did as well as fighting - trading far and wide and lending money. In the years that followed even monarchs came to them for financial assistance.

One such monarch, who would play a pivotal role in the orders demise was the king of France, Philip IV, known to history as Le Bel. Philip was an unpopular king, who had a hard time living up to the legacy of his ancestor, King Louis IX, or as we know him today Saint Louis. Le Bel, never did bridge the gap between himself and his illustrious ancestor, mainly because King Louis had never engaged in the sort of brutalities for which Philip was notorious.

Philip Le Bel was left with a huge debt by his father, the legacy of the Crusades. This combined with the country's war against England left the French coffers in a perpetual low state. So desperate was Le Bel to gain wealth, that he persecuted the Italian bankers (Lombards) and the Jews who lived in France, killing many and taking their wealth for the French cause. As if these atrocities were not enough, he recalled the French currency and melted it down, only to replace it with coins of lesser metal value. All of these acts, Philip IV undertook in the hopes of acquiring more and more wealth to aid his country and her war efforts.

There is an oft told tale that Philip Le Bel was mobbed in Paris by his own people, who no doubt would have strung him up, had it not been for his rescue and protection by the Knights Templar. It was in their Paris Preceptory that Le Bel probably fully realized the vast wealth possessed by the Templars and perhaps even developed the notion of coveting it for himself. It is likely that the arrest of the Templars was nothing more than another short term attempt to gain funds necessary to keep France afloat. However, in order to attack the Templars, Le Bel needed a plan. After all the Jews and Lombards were no opposition to the French armies. The Templars on the other hand, were powerful and need not answer to the king, being subservient only to the Pope. Since the Templars were responsible only to the Pope, part of Philip's plan was to create a Pope subservient to him. Clement V proved to be such a man.

Pope Clement V, was born Bertrand de Got and was the first in a long line of Popes to reside in Avignion France, rather than in Rome. Unlike many of the Popes before him, Clement was a weak and subservient Pope who constantly bowed to Philip Le Bel's every wish - including orchestrating the downfall of the Templar order. The authors Christopher Knight and Robert Lomas, in both, "The Hiram Key and their follow-up, "The Second Messiah", have uncovered evidence that Philip IV made six requests of Clement to ensure his position as Pope. Five of these were to be performed prior to his Papacy, and the sixth at a later date. It seems absurd that a mere monarch could set such provisions to a would be Pope, but it should be born in mind that Philip had almost certainly murdered one previous Pope and probably two. Knight and Lomas conclude that this sixth task to ensure Clement the Papal crown was the destruction of the Templars.

As stated earlier, that downfall commenced at dawn on Friday October 13th, 1307, which interestingly enough is the true reason why Friday the 13th still carries the superstition of sudden bad luck. Certainly this was the case for the Templars, caught apparently unaware and dragged off in chains to jails and prisons throughout France.

What followed was several years of interrogation, trials and confessions. These matters have been previously dealt with by many historians and will not be discussed again here except to say that, as Stephen uncovered while researching his first book on the Templars, "Unholy Worship", the accusations of Templar idolatry and demonic worship have prevailed to this day and have often been stitched into accusations against the modern Masonic fraternity.

The confessions of the Templars were largely gained at the crack of the torturer's whip and the interrogations, trials and tortures provided enough evidence for Pope Clement to issue two Papal bulls in March and May of 1312, dissolving the order. The first bull, "Vox in excelso" put forth, March 22nd, 1312 dealt with the actual dissolution and justifications therein. The second bull, "Ad Providam" came two months after on May 2, 1312 and claimed that the Templar wealth would be turned over to the order of the Hospital of St. John (the Hospitallers). The bull explained that the assets should be dedicated to the actual purpose for which they were donated in the first place and that the Hospitallers could aid that cause. History has shown, however, that little if any of the Templar wealth made it to the Hospitaller order. At the same time though, France began to see a steady economic recovery. Philip IV claimed that the French Crown took only the money that represented the costs of the Templar trials, though the truth is obviously less clear.

One would assume that with the disbanding of the order and subsequent distribution of assets, the Templar order had seen its end. Such was not immediately the case, for the last Grand Master of the Templars, Jacques de Molay remained in prison. De Molay had earlier confessed, along with other Templars, to idol worship and spitting on the Holy Cross, only later to recant his confessions. For this reason he was considered a relapsed heretic and on the morning of March 18th, 1314, along with fellow Templar, Geoffrey de Charney, he was taken to a small island on the Seine river and burned at the stake.

The story goes that De Molay stood proudly and defiantly against his captors claiming that he was guilty of but one crime - that of confessing untruths about his beloved order whilst under torture. As De Molay, clothed in nothing but his shirt, burned to death, he is claimed to have uttered a curse requesting both Philip and Clement to meet him before God within the year. True to the alleged curse, Philip died on April 20th, just one month later and Pope Clement on November 29th of the same year.

And so with the dissolution of the order of the Temple in 1312 and the martyrdom of its last Grand Master, Jacques de Molay, two years later in 1314, we come to the end of the story of the greatest monastic fighting order known to history......or do we?

Chapter Two

The Templar Treasure

N othing fascinates humanity more than the thought of finding some gleaming hoard of gold that has slept away the centuries undisturbed, to be happened upon by chance, assuring its finder of notoriety and wealth. This is the stuff of historical romance and most of us have thrilled to novels such as Robert Louis Stevenson's Treasure Island, or to real life accounts such as that of the discovery of the Royal tomb of Tutankhamun by Howard Carter in the 1920's. The German proto-archaeologist of the 19th century, Hienrich Schlieman, who had an almost fanatical interest in ancient Greek stories, used them as a basis to discover the true location of Troy, and became vastly wealthy as a result of his exertions on the hill of Hiserlik in modern Turkey.

As a logical extension of humanity's seemingly endemic attachment to treasure hoards, it is not at all surprising that the vastly wealthy Templars, apparently disappearing so fast from the European scene, have engendered any number of myths of their own. In terms of gold, silver and precious objects however, it is possible that humanity will be disappointed, for the reasons itemized below. But what might be infinitely more likely in the years ahead is the discovery of Templar treasure of a very different sort.

We have seen that the Templars were the first true bankers of Europe during a time when usury, the lending of money for interest was forbidden by the Church. There were, of course, other 'money lenders' about in the medieval period, and in regions where anti-Semitism was not operational, or temporarily subdued, an embryonic Jewish community within the states of Europe offered such a service, even to princes and kings. What made the Templars different was the sheer scale of their operation. For example, it would have been possible to deposit a sum of money in the Preceptory in Paris, where a ciphered deposit slip would be received, detailing exactly where one wished to redeem the amount. One could then travel to - say Bristol, and withdraw the money in the local currency - less interest of course. It was a bank and a Bureau de Change rolled into one. The advantages of such a system must have been self-evident. Travel was difficult and dangerous, with bandits frequenting many remote locations, so the Templars were offering a service that many people found admirable. In addition, the Templars were great lenders of money, sometimes on a huge scale. It is very probable that part of Philip Le Belle's reason for turning against the Templars was that he owed them such a great fortune in gold.

If we stop for a moment to consider the implications of these 'known facts' it must immediately become apparent that, to service such a network, Templar wealth, at least in terms of gold, must have been constantly redistributed throughout the many preceptories, and certainly the ones in the larger and more populous cities of Western Europe.

There is a marked difference between this and the way a medieval monarch would have dealt with cash. In England, for example, taxes were collected, ultimately for the King, along with revenues intended for the local lord of a place where one lived. Thus a proportion of the money paid over to a local bailiff or sheriff, would in turn be passed on up the line to the Crown.

Together with revenues from more wealthy lords, subject to his patronage and protection, the medieval king would probably be using such revenues very quickly but on those occasions where large amounts of money were accumulated, it would be kept in strong boxes, in defendable locations, such as royal castles. Medieval kings were powerful, but they weren't necessarily well educated and it is likely that a King such as Philip IV of France, seeing the opulence of the Templar establishment in Paris, would have assumed that somewhere in the bowels of such a building must be vast quantities of treasure.

A modern example might serve to show how wrong he probably was. A large multi national company can be worth billions of dollars on the stock exchanges of the world, but it is highly unlikely that even the most sumptuous board room would be the repository for anything more precious than pieces of paper, though its walls may be lined with valuable old masters.

Templar treasuries there will certainly have been, and their accumulated values must have been incredible, but it would have been economic and political suicide to keep one vast depository. It should also be mentioned that much of the Templar's wealth was constantly moving about, and was being used to make more money, thickening out the services on offer and expanding the business empire. The Templars owned vast areas of land in almost every Western European country, the accumulated revenues from which went to finance bigger and better ventures - and all run by a staff who were not paid in the general sense of the word, but whose efficiency was legendary. It is a fact of history that neither Philip IV, or anyone else, ever found the Templar treasure that was said to exist, though this may, in part, be due to the same sort of careful pre-planning that ensured the survival of the majority of Templar personnel. Just as surely as De Molay could take care of the brothers and servants of his order, in the ways outlined previously, so he must surely have ensured that movable wealth, in the form of treasure and objects, was spirited away to locations beyond the jurisdiction of the French Crown. Unfortunately, the Templars greatest asset - farm land, could

Dafoe and Butler in front of Rosslyn chapel, Roslin Scotland

not be moved, and this form of treasure, ultimately, did fall to either the Knights Hospitaller, or, in many cases, to the monarchs of Europe. Since the Templars, as a single institution, were outlawed in all Catholic countries, it is likely that a great proportion of their wealth passed to organizations which took their place, such as the Knights of Christ in Portugal, which we will examine in another chapter. But despite this self-evident fact, there must have been gold and silver in abundance within France itself. We have our own, very convincing, ideas regarding the ultimate home of this treasure, but as the reader will learn in due course, we do not believe that it is secreted in deep caves or even below the ancient stones of remote Templar churches.

However, there are enduring myths about Templar treasure, and one of these, relating to Oak Island in Canada, we will review at the end of this chapter, but for the moment we would wish to point out to the reader that there are many forms of 'treasure' and that not all of them gleam in the sun, as gold and silver would.

The Templars were the best sailors, the most efficient capitalists, the unparalleled builders and probably the most learned scholars of their day. We would suggest that herein lies the very treasure that Jacques de Molay would have wished to protect in 1307, which is just one of the reasons why four fifths of the French Templars were somehow smuggled out of France, or else moved to regions of the country where the crown could not find them. Eventually much of the Templar expertise did begin to disseminate and we will show how true this was with regard to maps, expertise in navigation and the general mathematical skills necessary to the explorer.

Neither can we dismiss the possibility that the Templars made some remarkable discoveries in Jerusalem, way back at the start of their adventure in Europe and the Holy Land. Legends abound of the Templars having found the Holy Grail, the Ark of the Covenant, the body of Christ, the head of John the Baptist, and any number of other less tangible treasures. Arguments for and against these assertions have filled so many books in recent years that we do not feel either empowered, or inclined, to discuss the possibilities in detail here. Nevertheless, at some level there could be a grain of truth in such rumors. According to the authors, Christopher Knight and Robert Lomas, whatever the Templars did find during their excavations of the Temple in Jerusalem, is presently residing below the stone floor of Rosslyn Chapel in Edinburgh. Knight and Lomas assert that this cache would contain documents relating to the true nature of Christianity and Biblical matters, and they are convinced that such a cache of treasure, precious beyond the dreams of avarice, are waiting to be found.

We may soon know, because the authors in question are presently seeking permission for archaeologists to lift the floor of Rosslyn Chapel and take a peek into the past. Whilst not demurring from the belief that such documents, and possibly even treasure of the metal variety, may once have laid below Rosslyn Chapel, we have to express our doubts that it would still be there. It is our avowed belief that there are still agencies abroad in Europe, and beyond, who know a great deal about such matters. As a result it is highly likely that the very discovery of these facts by Knight and Lomas may have been enough to ensure that any such cache is no longer in its former home of Rosslyn.

We now come to one of the most contentious, and yet the most popular, topic concerning possible Templar treasure, namely the little village of Rennes-Le-Chateau, in Southern France. For a complete discussion of the events relating to this village we would refer the reader to dozens of other books specifically geared to the topic, but in our estimation none deals with the matter in anywhere near as much detail as 'The Holy Blood and the Holy Grail', by Baigent, Leigh and Lincoln.

There is no doubt that this area of Southern France was a hotbed of Templarism. There were many Templar holdings in the area and the Blanchefort's, a family that had supplied one of the most successful Grand Masters of the order, lived close by. It seems that almost everyone has looked for treasure in this region, probably including the Templars themselves. The Visigoths, a people who had sacked the very city of Rome itself, had ruled the area in earliest times and were, themselves, said to have had a large treasury in the district. Perhaps the Templars found this wealth, and maybe, like everyone since, they did not. But the theme is an enduring one, and whether the treasure was that of the Visigoths, or the Templars, even the forces of the German High Command searched the area extensively during the Second World War. Personally we remain open-minded about the whole complicated business. Perhaps we will never know the secrets allegedly held by the mountains of Rennes-

Le-Chateau, but as frequently as the areas of this small village have been examined, it is a small island on the other side of the Atlantic, which has attracted a great deal of interest in regards to the supposed Templar treasure.

Oak Island is a 140 acre island located in Mahone Bay off the eastern coast of Nova Scotia. It is not the island itself that attracts the attention but rather the so called Money Pit it is said to contain. The Oak island story begins in 1795 when Daniel McGinnis, a teenage boy, was wandering the small island. McGinnis came across a circular depression in the ground - a small sink hole of sorts. What caught his interest was the fact that situated over the hole was a tree, which for all appearances seemed to be notched out for a block and tackle rig. Now being of a young impressionable age and no doubt in knowledge of the legends of pirates having been in the area, Daniel immediately assumed that this was the spot so often marked on a pirate's map with an X.

With the assistance of some friends, McGinnis spent considerable time digging in the pit, to try and discover the treasure that surely the hole contained. They were able to get to a depth of thirty feet, but found no treasure. It was not to be touched for another eight years when the boys, then men, would return along with a company set up to aid in uncovering the treasure contained. The new dig was able to take them three times their original depth, to a level of ninety feet, but still no treasure.

From that dig in 1803 to modern times, there have been as many digs into the money pit as there have been theories as to what may be buried there and by whom. Theories ranging from the sublime to the ridiculous have included the obvious notion of Pirate treasures, the treasures of William Kidd and even a rather far fetched notion that the original plays of Shakespeare, were buried there by Francis Bacon, who wrote them since Shakespeare was essentially illiterate. But these theories, while very interesting to the seeker of treasures, are not the province of this book, save for one.

A notion that is gaining some followers is that the Templars took their vast wealth of gold, silver and jewels and carried it across the Atlantic to bury it in a two hundred foot deep pit. The theory goes on to claim, that only the architectural knowledge of the Templars would have the intellect to construct the elaborate irrigation system that allowed the pit to flood every time someone attempted to gain entrance to it. While the thought of Templar architectural abilities having a hand in the construction does seem more in keeping with logic than the notion that such a clever booby trap was engineered by a band of pirates, we must contend that the idea that the Templars would bury their treasure is simply ridiculous. We come to this conclusion on the basis of pure economics and the capitalism that was espoused by the order.

As we saw in an earlier chapter, after the fall of Acre in 1291, an important date to our own research and theories as will be evidenced in a later chapter, the Templars returned to their preceptories throughout Europe. Here, with no more Holy wars to wage, they fell back on their second career, finance. As history has shown, and quite soundly so, the capitalistic lending of money, combined with the order being the proverbial scapegoat in the loss of the Holy Land, was largely the catalyst for their losing the favor of the European populace. Still from the years of 1291 to their arrest in 1307, Templar Inc. continued to profit from the lending of money to Lords and monarchs alike. As we mentioned earlier, one of those monarchs was Philip Le Bel, whom may have closed in on the order in order to default on his loan.

If we compare the Templar Banking system to any modern bank, for most assuredly that is what they were well before their time, we will accept that most of the Templar wealth was out in the field, earning interest and revenue for the order. Now suddenly at dawn, October 13th, 1307, the order is effectively shut down. What then becomes of the money that is out working and earning interest as loans? It is lost and never repaid. We have no doubt that Jacques de Molay had advanced notice of the arrest. We know that the arrest orders were dated September 14th, so at the most they had four weeks advanced notice. Any attempt at a wholesale effort to recollect all of the outstanding loans, certainly would have sent off alarms that the knowledge of their imminent arrest was in the Templar's hands.

So rather than run the risk of blowing their cover, we theorize that Templar Inc. did what any good business would do in a similar financial crisis, it cut its losses and moved on. With a depleted stockpile of workable assets, coinage, gold, jewels and other salable goods, the Templars fled the area of immediate persecution, before the hammer could fall. Did the Templars go west across the Atlantic with the only remaining working capital left in their care, only to bury it in the ground on a remote island? What would the motive have been other than an attempt to spite the King of France? Perhaps that was the case, but it remains highly unlikely when it is understood that this group of former warriors had in the years after Acre, essentially traded in their weapons, in exchange for an abacus. To draw a more modern comparison, suppose a major bank suddenly was forced to shut down several branches. Would the CEO of the bank take the deposits of those branches and hide them in his mattress or in a shoe box hidden in the rafters? We would argue that this would never occur. In reality, the money would be transferred to those branches still open and put to even greater use to recover the recent losses. We are of the firm opinion that, that is essentially what the Templars did with what wealth remained at their disposal.

Although we have scanned the published material relating to the supposed end of the Templar order very closely, it remains a puzzle to us why successive 'experts' have built their theories regarding the supposed existence of Templar treasure around notions that would surely have been alien to the very ethos of the institution they are studying.

In ending this chapter on Templar treasure, we would wish to point out once more, that we do believe emphatically that Templar wealth existed, and that it was taken, probably in small amounts, so as not to engender suspicion, in the weeks prior to October 1307, to a number of specific locations. One region, in particular, seems to offer the most tangible proof of almost complete Templar survival, and we will be describing this in detail. But we are forced to conclude that the very legacy of the Templars, their economic innovation, engineering, navigation and exploration, and probably even their deepest held beliefs, represent the greatest Templar treasure of them all. Alan's book, The Grail and the Rose, should demonstrate these facts admirably, and this writing partnership also has much more to say concerning these matters in the months and years that lie ahead.

Of the specific sites mentioned, Rosslyn Chapel seems to be the most likely candidate for Templar secrets, though we content ourselves with the fact that the building's very fabric, its fabulous carvings and its geographical positioning contribute to a Templar storehouse of treasure that may take decades to decode. We further assert that the bulk of Templar treasure is indeed waiting to be discovered, but we personally doubt that much of it would find a ready home in an 'assay office' for as sure as 'all that glistens is not gold' the reverse is often true and very weathered stones of several hundred Templar buildings may, collectively, offer one of the greatest treasures the world has ever known. Once we discover the language - a time that draws ever closer - then the true fortune of the Knights Templar will be ours.

Chapter Three

The Fate Of The Fleet

A nd so we come to one of the most mysterious, and therefore probably the most pawed over, aspect of the destruction of the Knights Templar, namely, what happened to the Templar fleet of ships, which is said to have been moored in La Rochelle immediately prior to October 13th, 1307.

It occurs to us, once again, that frequently researchers into the Templar order have begun by asking question that may not be entirely relevant. For example, everyone has assumed that the entire Templar fleet was in the Atlantic French port of La Rochelle at the time of Philip le Bel's attack on the order. However, it stands as self evident that if there is absolutely no information as to where the ships went, probably sometime on Thursday October 12th, neither is there any record of the actual number of ships involved in the operation. The number of ships to leave La Rochelle has been argued by many to have been eighteen galleys. This is due to the testimony of Jean de Chalon, who stated during the trials that the Paris Preceptor, Gerard de Villiers had escaped with fifty horses and eighteen ships. We have argued extensively through this book that it is very likely that the Templar commanders had a very good idea what was about to happen to them and we have stressed that the leaders of this organization were just as clever, and probably considerably more so, than Philip IV of France and his fellow monarchs in Europe.

Taking all these matters into consideration we arrive at a number of observations that must be made before any discussion of the missing Templar Fleet can take place.

It has been suggested by several researchers that De Molay was completely ignorant of the imminent arrest, due to the fact that just the day before the raids, he acted as pall bearer for King Philip's sister in law. This one small act seems to be enough evidence for those authors to contend a complete lack of knowledge of the forthcoming events on Molay's part. We would disagree with this.

Indeed Philip had called De Molay to Paris, to keep him close at hand. But to do anything less than to comply with Philip's wishes would have been for Jacques de Molay to telegraph his own, intimate, knowledge of what lay ahead. It is even possible that De Molay had every intention of allowing himself to be arrested. We base this assertion on the knowledge that the very rule of the Templar order commanded the brothers to defend one another and, as Grand Master, it was Jacques de Molay's duty to protect the order, at the cost of his own life if necessary. However, it is possible that Molay, though being aware that arrest was imminent, probably did not expect to be tortured or killed. He probably assumed that his incarceration would be short lived and that, in any case, he would be best able to defend his men if he was close to the accusers.

If Jacques de Molay, Grand Master of the Templars in 1307, had known the organization was going to be attacked, he would also have been aware that the first possible route of escape for his personnel that the French authorities would observe closely would be La Rochelle.

Only 620 Templar personnel are known to have been arrested in France in the days and weeks following the 1307 attack. The authors Michael Baigent and Richard Leigh estimate that there were over 3,000 Templars of one sort or another in France in 1307. Incredibly then, only one fifth of the French Templars were ever apprehended. Imagine then, as many researchers seemed to have failed to do, the comprehension of over 2,000 fully armed and equipped Templar brothers, with their entire retinues of squires, servants, horses, baggage trains and camp followers, issuing forth from all parts of France in the days prior to October 13th, and all making their way to La Rochelle. Philip IV could not have failed to have sentries mounted on the roads to the port and would have known immediately if such an exodus was taking place, in which case he would surely have shown his hand earlier, and stopped the mass movement.

It is no doubt appealing, if only for the sake of the enduring mystery, which itself is so intriguing, to imagine several dozen cargo ships, escorted by armed galleons, issuing forth from La Rochelle and, banners flying, sailing majestically into history - but it simply cannot have happened in this way. If such a large fleet had sailed south, to Portugal, or Southern Spain, somebody would have reported the fact. If, as Baigent and Leigh imply, the bulk of the ships had circumnavigated Southern England and the west coast of Ireland before making landfall off the west coast of Scotland, Edward of England, who had regular patrols in these sea-ways, could not have failed to have been aware. In fact only if the entire fleet, having first eluded the specifically vigilant forces of Philip of France, had headed due west into the sunset of Thursday October 12th, 1307, could it have so neatly disappeared from the annals of history.

This latter scenario should not be dismissed out of hand. There are tales relating that the great Templar wealth came, in part, from silver mined in Central America and shipped back to Europe, and since later transatlantic voyages were obviously in possession of Templar charts, it is almost certain that the Templars themselves did cross the Atlantic, probably regularly. But even assuming that the Templars were very familiar with the eastern seaboard of America, it is highly unlikely that such a large fleet could have made landfall anywhere on the coastal seaboard of what is now the United States or America, without some mention of it passing into the traditions of the indigenous peoples of the region.

In the case of the Aztecs, whose vast civilization based on Mexico, was reaching its zenith in 1307, there are enduring tales of a white god who came from the east and brought civilization to the region, but such stories were ancient when the Spanish arrived in the region, only a century and a half after the supposed Templar exodus. Bearing in mind the very advanced technology of the Templars, together with their tremendous fighting skill, a Templar fleet of the size envisaged would most certainly have affected the entire Aztec civilization to an incredible degree.

On the other hand, it is just conceivable that the Templars made landfall in some more remote place, or even much further north in Canada. However, it is equally difficult to explain how such a massive influx of Europeans could have either perished without any tangible trace, or failed to leave a noticeable mark on the local landscape, prior to the arrival of other Europeans in the new world in the 15th century. There are unexplained European settlements on the east coast of America, such as the one discovered (and probably known about) by the Pilgrim Fathers, close to Cape Cod, but the indications are that this abandoned site, and probably others, had been limited affairs, or else surely they must have survived in some shape or form. Back on the European side of the Atlantic the thought of the entire Templar fleet hauling up in Scotland is equally preposterous. Even if the ships could have avoided the gaze of Philip in France, and the ships of King Edward in the Channel, it is even more doubtful that some chronicler or other would have known of the mass arrival and yet failed to write a word about it.

We don't doubt that Templar knights assisted Robert the Bruce in his struggle against the English, and especially in Bannockburn in 1314, but such an eventuality need not have involved a single French Templar knight. The Templar order was extremely strong in Scotland itself, which was its natural British home from the very inception of the order. It was even stronger in England, where the vacillating tendencies of King Edward II, who showed no real, personal desire to attack the Knights Templar, would have allowed the vast majority to slip quietly across the Scottish border. In fact, without wishing to appear flippant, if all the missing French, English and Scottish Templar knights had arrayed their forces in front of the English at Bannockburn in 1314, we doubt that the English would have remained on the field long enough to fire a single arrow! Of course all of this assumes that the French Templars could have disembarked from the 500 Templar preceptories of France without Philip realizing that anything was happening.

For all these reasons we are forced to conclude that one of the greatest mysteries of the Templars - the missing fleet, is probably not a mystery at all.   Time and again we have come across evidence that previous researchers into this field have singularly failed to bear in mind regarding the nature of the Templar order by 1307. The Templars were a progressive faction, dynamic and constantly thrusting into new markets, searching out mercantile opportunities, and ever growing in strength. Degenerate the order may have become in some ways, for example personal adherence to the vows of the order, but there is absolutely no proof that the institution as a whole was crumbling. Under these circumstances it would not make sense to keep a huge fleet, with the manpower that it demanded, constantly in port, just in case of an eventuality that may or may not come to pass. As we have noted in other chapters, after the fall of Acre, the Templars went back to their secondary interests in commerce. Therefore we are certain that these ships did not stay moored, but rather continued to sail and promote the financial and mercantile interests of Templar Inc.

So, where was the Templar fleet in October 1307? Undoubtedly there were ships moored in La Rochelle, and probably a reasonably large number. But the vast majority of Templar ships, both merchant vessels and armed galleons, would surely have been doing what the Templars did best -plying the seas of the Mediterranean and the Atlantic, earning money to keep the order financially sound. We can see clearly that the Templars exemplified an embryonic belief in a form of capitalism that was diametrically opposed to the stultified view of monarchs such as Philip IV of France. And of course if we continue to view the Templars through his eyes, we will inevitably be left with the conception of a huge army of men, and a vast fleet of ships, simply waiting for the next pitched battle. Even medieval monarchs only gathered a standing army together when there was a need to fight because they simply could not afford to have thousands of men at arms sitting around doing nothing for most of the time. As we have clearly demonstrated, the modus operandi of the Templars had changed markedly since the loss of the Holy Land and so, by 1307, it had become Templar Inc. It could move goods and people effectively from one place to another, and it could protect them from interference of Muslim forces or from pirates; it could guard roads and move sums of money and goods around all over Europe, ensuring that such pack trains were safe from local bandits. But all of these things could only be achieved because the Templars were constantly monitoring the state of their huge empire. By 1307 they were far from being the single, entire, standing army of the sort that had fought pitched battles in the Levant. If Jacques de Molay had known what lay in store for the order in 1307, and the fact that ships did manage to slip their moorings in La Rochelle and escape the clutches of the French Crown surely proves that he did, he could never have been so stupid as to make the express move that the slower reasoning Philip expected.

We see the most likely scenario as follows: Jacques de Molay was coming under pressure to form an alliance between the Templar order and that of the Knights Hospitaller, pressure that he was staunchly resisting. An order of which, we feel compelled to add, Philip Le Bel sought to be the Rex Bellator or War King of. De

Molay knew the way the political tide was turning against his order, and he may have been deeply suspicious that he had been called to France in the autumn of 1307. We can assume that what befell him was no great surprise. If, however, he had refused to come to France, he would have incurred the wrath of both Philip le Bel and Pope Clement. More importantly, his actions would have shown that he was well aware of the impending storm and his failure to visit France at such a crucial time would have telegraphed his comprehension of what was to come, probably spurring Philip into action before the Templars were fully organized.

In all probability carefully laid plans were put into operation prior to his arrival in France. Slowly but surely, and in dozens of ways, Templar knights would have moved from their preceptories, eventually taking routes to safety ahead of the final assault in October. On no occasion would the exodus have been allowed to become so great that any suspicions were aroused in Paris. Some Templars were probably disguised, as merchants dealing with the order, whilst others may have taken on the persona of ordinary civilians. In this way most of the preceptories outside of Paris could have been reduced to a skeleton staff, who were deliberately left behind to keep Philip busy in the days after the dawn raids of October 1307.

With regard to La Rochelle, it is highly likely that both men and goods were transshipped from the port, some to Portugal, others to Spain, and still others to parts of Ireland or Scotland, but this was a process that could easily have taken weeks, and once again deliberately planned so that no suspicions should be aroused. We hope to show presently where the bulk of the Templars actually went, but with our combined knowledge of the order, we do not suggest that they traveled anywhere 'en masse'. And the result of this gradual exodus answers another question we could not fail to ask ourselves: Why did the Templar preceptories not fight back on October 13th? The simple answer to this question must surely be that there were not enough knights left in any of the preceptories in France to constitute a viable fighting force.

We buttress these conclusions with one overwhelming piece of evidence. If Philip le Bel did take both Jacques de Molay and his order completely by surprise, as many historians are still asserting, why were only one fifth of the French Templars ever arrested? We do know of at least one instance where our theories can be substantiated. Two Templar Knights from the Paris Preceptory, or one very close to it, were captured soon after the fateful day, at Chaumont, which is on the very edge of what was then French territory, only a few miles from safety. And, with its position in Eastern France, this is exactly the direction that we would have expected the escaping knights to have taken.

In our conception De Molay's plan was clever and subtle, though it did involve sacrificing the entire staff of the Paris Preceptory and a proportion of the Templars as a whole to the Inquisition - and from the very start he probably realized that this unfortunate number must include himself.

It is certain that the moorings at La Rochelle were bereft of ships at dawn on Friday October 13th, 1307, and it is very likely that De Molay had ensured that there were at least enough craft present until that time to allay any fears on Philip's part. But if by 'the Templar Fleet' we are intended to think in terms of the bulk of the Templar ships, replete with a large proportion of the Templar knights of France, we are forced to conclude that, although the idea is deeply romantic and highly attractive, it is almost certainly false. The remaining ships slipped anchor in the days approaching October 13th, the events of which Jacques de Molay probably comprehended from the moment the plans were laid, for he must surely have maintained spies amongst the highest echelons of Philip's advisers. No messenger of Philip's from La Rochelle could have traveled to Paris in less than two days, even allowing for constant riding and strings of horses along the route - leaving plenty of time for any remaining ships to out maneuver the French King. From La Rochelle they would have split up, according to careful instructions, and small groups would have made landfall in a number of different places.

In closing this chapter we fully concede that our conceptions of the events of October 13th, 1307 are a radical departure from orthodoxy regarding these matters. But it is worth reiterating that sticking to established historical dogmas regarding all matters relating to the Templars may promote a deeper and deeper sense of mystery and awe regarding the white knights, but it does little to try and address real events and their consequences.

We hope we have demonstrated that France was probably bereft of most of its Knights Templar personnel by the time October

1307 arrived, though we are fully conversant with the theory that many of the Templar knights found a safe haven in isolated parts of Southern France and we do not dispute that, to a limited degree, this may have been the case. And as for the vast fleet of the Templars, all components of which must have come to port at some stage after the day of horrors instituted by Philip IV. The Mediterranean was replete with ports where the Templars would be welcomed with open arms, long after the initial French attacks. Most of the Templar merchant and fighting fleet was undoubtedly absorbed by Templar fraternities that survived the destruction of the Mother order. There, under different names and slightly altered flags, they must have continued to serve the overall strategy of Jacques de Molay, who though languishing in a Paris prison could at least be satisfied that he had out maneuvered, out witted and completely wrong footed the vain and self-seeking Philip le Bel of France.

Chapter Four

The Retreat To Scotland

P robably the most enduring theme concerning the fate of the Templars, and certainly the most topical at this time, is that of a wholesale emigration of French Templars after 1307 to Scotland. There is a vast repository of evidence to substantiate claims that a large number of Templar knights did in fact find their way to the northernmost part of the British Isles, and also sound reasons for their actions. Templarism was endemic to Scotland, and had been from the very start of the organization. History relates that Hughes de Payens, the first Grand Master of the Templars, was married to Catherine St. Clair, who was the niece of Baron Henri St. Clair of Roslin. The first Templar establishment to be built outside of either France or the Holy Land, was founded on Sinclair land. Today the village of Temple, south east of Edinburgh, is a sleepy little place, but at the bottom of the steep hill that marks the main street of the present village one can still see the ruins of ecclesiastical buildings, nestling in their tree hung hollow, by the little stream that once served the community.

The Templars came to have many holdings in Scotland and were ever close to the Royal rulers of the country and this was still the case on that fateful day in 1307. For a while the Crown of Scotland was held in English hands but soon after this there came a time when, Robert the Bruce was maintaining a precarious hold on the Scottish throne. Robert the Bruce, though now synonymous with Scottish pride and independence, was certainly no Scot by ancestry. He was, like most rulers of his day, of Norman origins, his family having arrived in England with William the Conqueror in 1066. But the Bruce's had fallen out with the English crown back in the days of King John, and had fared better under Scottish patronage after this time.

There is much to indicate that Robert the Bruce may have maintained more than a passing interest in Templarism. Although the whole length of his adult life was committed to the Scottish cause, which meant a constant battle with England, he had strong Crusader and Templar leanings. So much so that at his death he had left instructions that his heart should be taken on Crusade, and buried in Jerusalem. This task was undertaken by Sir William de St. Clair and Sir James Douglas, though unfortunately Robert's heart got no further than Spain, and was eventually returned to Scotland, to reside to this day in Melrose Abbey.

It has been suggested for some decades that Templars fleeing from the tyranny of the French attack upon them, were to be found fighting by the side of Robert the Bruce, against the English, at the Battle of Bannockburn on June 24th, 1314, only seven short years after the 1307 watershed. Although there is no historical records of this Templar involvement, it has come to be accepted as fact by many. This largely due to the fact that the English were routed by the Scots in this battle and it is more or less certain that the white clad knights of the Templars were instrumental in turning the tide of the battle. It is now becoming popular to assume that the missing Templar fleet, leaving France just a day or two before October 13th, 1307, sailed around the southern coast of England, circumnavigating Ireland, before making landfall on the West Coast of Scotland, which was an area in the personal control of Robert the Bruce.

The authors Baigent and Leigh discovered a Templar graveyard, and therefore a community, in Argyllshire that had been in constant use from the thirteenth to the eighteenth century and there are a large number of megalithic monuments in the area that are still known today as 'The Temple Wood Complex' bearing testimony to the original ownership and control of this land.

It is possible however, that the notions of a 'mass exodus' of Templars from France to Scotland are overplayed. There was a strong Templar presence in the country from long before 1307, and probably more than enough to account for the Argyllshire survival into comparatively recent times. The late Masonic historian, Albert Mackay, claimed that a papal inquisition was held at Hollyrood in 1309, at which only two Templars showed up. It was his belief, based on his research at the time, that the Scottish Templars left and offered their services to Robert the Bruce.

Doubtless, the Bruce would have welcomed extra Templar

fighters to his beleaguered land after 1307, and at least at first, he had little to fear from the Pope regarding threats of excommunication if he failed to persecute the Templars himself, as King Edward had been forced to do in England. Robert the Bruce was fighting for the very survival of Scotland as an independent entity, and had he fallen into English hands his life would have been worth little. A reliance on the Templars during such fearful times for Scotland would have made eminent sense. Scotland was far away from the guiding hand of Rome, and Robert cared little for orthodox religion, but in our estimation King Robert may, in the end, have found himself faced with the same sort of potential threats that worried Philip Le Bel of France so much, namely that too many Templars in one's kingdom could prove a curse in times of peace, no less than the blessing they represented when armed men were required. If the Templars really were as strong in the region as we have been led to believe, even Robert, with his own deeply entrenched respect for the Templars, may have seen them as posing a potential problem to his own dynasty. And so, probably somewhat reluctantly, a later and more secure King Robert nominally fell in line with the European actions regarding the Templars, though there is absolutely no evidence that a single Templar knight was ever persecuted 'north of the Border'.

At   least one   major strand of Templarism certainly prevailed in Scotland and this was that espoused and championed by what may have been one of the oldest Templar families of them all - the Sinclairs. Mentioned elsewhere in this book, and originally having been St. Clair, from France, the Sinclairs had been in Scotland from an extremely early date, though they too had first arrived in England with William I. It was a member of this extremely powerful family, Henry Sinclair, who made the now quite famous trip to the New World, just a short time after the Templar persecutions in Europe. And it was Henry's grandson, William Sinclair, who was responsible for building the extraordinary Rosslyn Chapel.

Rosslyn Chapel stands on Templar land south of Edinburgh. It is a sacred place to Freemasons throughout the world, who seem to instinctively recognize within its Gothic construction and elaborate carvings, the precedents of their own particular beliefs. Certainly the Chapel owes little to being a church in the conventional sense, and our own discoveries, in addition to a wealth of information from other directions, shows it to be the location where Templarism spawned Freemasonry.

The most likely explanation is that Henry Sinclair, just over a century after the fall of the European Templars, wished to construct an edifice that would somehow 'reflect' the earliest achievement of the Templars, namely their excavation of Solomon's Temple on the sacred mound in Jerusalem. The authors Knight and Lomas have demonstrated that Rosslyn Chapel, supposedly never completed, was, in reality, always intended to appear unfinished, since it is meant to be a medieval representation of what the part of Solomon's Temple excavated by the Templars at the start of the 12th century probably looked like. If this assumption is true, then it is quite obvious that at least by the middle of the 15th century, when Rosslyn Chapel was being built, Templarism was far from dead in Scotland.

The connection between Scottish Rite Freemasonry and the Knights Templar is, for reasons which we find somewhat difficult to understand, a contentious one. Certainly officers and representatives of English Freemasonry at Grand Lodge in London, still deny a connection between the two institutions, preferring to suggest that Freemasonry only really began in the 18th century. In our estimation, and with ample evidence to prove the point, this is patently not the case, since Masonic type Lodges of one sort or another are traceable in Scotland almost right back to the time of the building of Rosslyn Chapel. There are several documents know to Masons that date to a much earlier time than the Grand Lodge of England's, supposed date of 1717. One of these would involve the Kilwinning Lodge in Scotland, which is said to date back to 1670 and the Halliwell Manuscript is said to date to 1390. Exactly why Grand Lodge in London maintains its seemingly pointless claims is a great puzzle. The most likely explanation for the commencement of Freemasonry is tied up with the political realities of Europe in the 15th and 16th centuries. The Templars were universally outlawed, and as we have seen, even Scotland had to fall in line with Catholic edicts to this effect.

But to a family such as the Sinclairs, steeped in Templar tradition, this state of affairs was simply unacceptable. It is suggested that there were certain 'secrets' locked into the design of, and probably buried below Rosslyn Chapel. These assertions are born out by Alan's research into the sacred nature of Gothic architecture and by the strategic positioning of Rosslyn Chapel. The Chapel occupies a position on a line of longitude exactly 39 megalithic degrees from Jerusalem (see The Bronze Age Computer Disc by Alan Butler). In addition, the Grand Circle distance between Jerusalem and Rosslyn Chapel is 'exactly' 1/10th of the Earth's circumference, which in modern terms would be expressed as 2,160 nautical miles. In megalithic terms this would be 2,196 Megalithic miles, because megalithic geometry works on a base of 366 degrees, rather than the more common 360 degrees. It is at 1/10th of the circumference of the Earth that the modern system of Nautical Miles and the ancient system of Megalithic miles are harmoniously reconciled. Alan has shown elsewhere that the Templars, as legatees of the ancient mathematics, were fully conversant with its wonderful aids to navigation. We respectfully submit that the positioning of Rosslyn Chapel is hardly likely to be a random chance event, and particularly unlikely bearing in mind that Rosslyn is said to be a copy of Solomon's Temple which was in Jerusalem. These facts, together with what William Sinclair may have hidden below Rosslyn Chapel, represented information that the Sinclairs would not have wished to pass on to the uninitiated, not least of all because it gave the Sinclairs, and the post Templar mariners, a definite advantage in navigation. As a result William was forced to invent some way of securing the secrecy of those taking part in the building of his Chapel.

Using aspects of Templar belief and worship, William Sinclair created a 'secret society' to which his stonemasons were introduced. Ultimately, what started out as a form of 'charter' assuring the masons of continued patronage and exclusive privileges regarding their trade, became a world wide institution of a 'speculative' rather than a 'practical' sort. We do not want to labor the Masonic point in this chapter, because we have dealt with it more fully elsewhere, but it seems evident enough to us that the precepts of Freemasonry owe much to the survival of Templar and post Templar thinking in Scotland.

The stories of the Templar fleet, in its entirety, having fled France to take up refuge in Scotland, may be based on circumstantial evidence and even 'wish fulfillment' in the minds of Templar motivated Freemasons of the present era, for there is no historical corroboration of the event. However, the fleet certainly went somewhere, and Scotland may have been as likely as any other destination. What is evident is that the Templar ideals were so deeply entrenched in the running of Scotland at the highest level, that at least some aspects of its precepts and organization remained within the Kingdom until very recent times - and for all anyone can say, might be still enshrined in uniquely Scottish beliefs that may or may not resurface if Scottish independence ever becomes a reality.

Chapter Five

The Portuguese Years

M any who have read accounts of how Templars, fleeing the French oppression of 1307, set the fleet towards Portugal where they joined the newly formed "Order of Christ" are left with the impression that the "Order of Christ" had been established with the express objective of offering sanctuary to the Templars. In reality the Knights Templar had already held a strong presence in the Iberian peninsula for many years prior to 1307 and the arrest of the French brethren.

In 1128, just one year after the order received its rule at the Council of Troyes, Teresa of Portugal gave the newly formed knights the town of Fonte Arcada. This gift was not entirely altruistic or as compensation for Portugal being unwilling to take up the Crusaders cross. For the Templars there was indeed a price to be paid which was to help win back territories previously occupied by the Moors. This, the brethren did with the zeal and military skill that has become synonymous with the warrior monks.

From the period of 1143-1190, the Knights Templar presence in Portugal became stronger by the year. The castle of Langrovia was donated by Fernao Mendes and his wife the Infanta Sancha Henrique, who was the sister of King Henrique, and with whom Templars had worked in previous times. Later in 1159, the order was granted Castle Ceras, which was, at the time, little more than a ruin. The Portuguese Templar Master, Gualdim Pais decided to construct a new fortress in the area, which he commenced one year later in 1160. This fortress was to be built in nearby Tomar. This particular piece of Templar architecture survives to this day and is not only a principle tourist attraction in Portugal, but is considered by many to be both a mystical and spiritual place.

The castle itself is known by the name, "Convento de Cristo" and remains an impressive epitaph to Templar abilities in architecture. Within its ancient fortifications lies an eight sided chapel, which was a standard style of Templar architecture. This octagonal form of building which the Templars are believed to have developed from the Muslim's "Dome of the Rock" in Jerusalem, served a threefold objective to the Templar masons. Firstly its eight walls formed a superior edifice of structural stability. Secondly it called to mind the overall shape of the Templar Cross Patee, which can be easily formed within the confines of the octagon. Finally, the octagon, especially when combined within the circle, formed a sacred geometry associated with Gnostic beliefs, for which the Knights Templar were said to share an affinity. It is rumored that within this octagonal chapel, called a "Charola", neophyte Templar knights were initiated on horseback.

Another related mystical Templar holding is close to Tomar. This is the Church of Santa Maria do Olivel, considered by the Portuguese to be the Mother Church of all the churches in Africa, Asia and even the America's. Its most striking aspect is the large window on its front facade adorned with a rosette containing the Templar Sigil. At Santa Maria do Olivel is buried the body of Master Gauldim Pais, who founded Tomar as a Templar province. But Tomar would not be the end of the Templar expansion in Portugal. Nine years later the order was allowed to retain a full third of all lands captured   south of the Tagus. During this period it was confirmed that the Portuguese Templars owned the castles of Tomar, Cardiga and Foz do Zezere. In reality the ownership of these locations would prove to be a moot point in 1314, when King Dinis would claim them for himself.

In general, the Portuguese Templar position continued to grow and remain stable throughout the reigns of Afonso I and II, right on to that of King Sancho III. It was not until the reign of Afonso III, that the Templars began to carry less favor in the eyes of the Portuguese Monarchy. The reasons for this decline in esteem are sketchy at best and not particularly pertinent to our story, and in any case it was a later Portuguese king who would prove pivotal during the true decline of the Templars in 1307.

This monarch was King Dinis I (1279-1325) who achieved much on behalf of his country. Dinis' promotion of agriculture earned him the name, "The Farmer", while his love of literature, especially poetry, of which he is said to have written volumes, was perhaps his reason for establishing a university at Lisbon. Dinis was instrumental in the growth of industry within Portugal forming a commercial treaty with King Edward I of England in 1294. Politically, Dinis was perhaps most noted for his work against the military orders, especially the order of Santiago, which, within his territory, he was able to bring under Portuguese control. It was this same spirit that would work to his advantage during the persecution of the Templars by Philip Le Bel and Clement V.

We demonstrated at the start of this book that the fall of the Templars began with the arrest of the French brethren on October 13th, 1307. However, King Dinis, in common with his trading partner, King Edward of England, did not believe the accusations made against the Templars, although the papal bull, "Regnas In Coelis", written in 1308 ordered the heads of all Catholic countries to fully investigate the order. Eventually Edward of England bowed to the whims of Pope Clement and arrested the English Templars, imprisoning the English Grand Master in the Tower of London, where he later died. King Dinis, however did not arrest the brethren in his lands, but spent two years investigating the order as his response to the Papal request. To what degree he genuinely examined the order remains a matter of conjecture, but the Pope is said to have written a letter in 1310 to the Kings of Portugal, Castile, Leon and Aragon complaining that not enough torture was being used in their 'inquiries': He maintained:

"The Bishops and delegates, have imprudently neglected these means of obtaining the truth; we therefore expressly order them to employ torture against the Knights, that the truth may be more readily and completely obtained"

Later that year a joint policy was issued between Portugal and neighboring Castile, which found the Knights Templar innocent of all crimes on Iberian lands. So it seemed that the Templars would be allowed to continue in the Iberian territories, unhindered by the long arm of the Holy See. However, this was not the case, as another Papal bull was issued in 1312, which hit a little closer to the coffers of the King of Portugal. Clement's bull, "Ad Providam", which we looked at in chapter one, bequeathed all Templar holdings to the rival order of St. John. It is at this point in history, that King Dinis turned from protector of the Templar knights, to protector of his own political interests. Dinis argued with the Pope that the lands occupied by the Templars did not truly belong to the order, but rather they were only granted perpetual use of the properties. Ownership of the forts, castles and chapels, he asserted, properly belonged to the Portuguese crown and that crown belonged to King Dinis himself. It was for this reason and perhaps no other that Dinis formed his own religious and military order which he named "The Order of Christ."

Several years after the conversion, on march 14th, 1319, Pope John XXII issued the papal bull, "Ad ea exquibis", which confirmed the new order of knighthood. This Pope became the order's patron and interestingly enough gave it a Cistercian rule, which had also been granted to the Templars two centuries before. Soon after the papal sanction, the order expanded its activities into Spain, Italy, Germany and its former home France. All Templar holdings including the city of Tomar were transferred to the Order of Christ, which chose the Church of Santa Maria do Castelo as its first headquarters under the leadership of its first Grand Master, Gil Martins. Martins had already been the master of the Order of Avis and so was always a likely candidate to head Dinis' new order. Martins' past experience with military orders was probably the catalyst that allowed the order to quickly expand to 69 knights by 1321. Additionally the fledgling order had nine chaplains, six sergeants, a Grand Prior, Grand Commander and the standard bearer which was called "the Alferes."

That standard would prove to be similar to, but not identical with, the Cross Patee of the Templar knights. Like the Patee, it was a blood red cross of equal arms, each of which flared out forming an octagon shape. In addition the cross of the Order of Christ contained a twist of silver in the middle of its body. It is this modified Templar cross that many readers will recall from childhood history books, emblazoned on the sails of explorer's ships. Indeed many of the first oceanic navigators were members of, or learned their craft from, this newly established order. The Knights of Christ had, in turn, gained its expertise in seamanship from the Templars who had transported, pilgrims, warriors and goods from Europe to the Holy Lands, centuries earlier.

One of those explorers was the famous Prince Henry the Navigator, who is not to be confused with Prince Henry St. Clair of Roslin, a man we will look at again in the next chapter. Prince Henry of Portugal was born in 1394, the third son of King Joao I. At the age of twenty, Prince Henry, accepted by historians as a devoutly religious man, persuaded his father to embark on a Crusade against the Muslim port of Ceuta, on the northern coast of Africa. The purpose of this Crusade was to bring the faith of Jesus Christ to all the Muslim souls wishing salvation. Legend has it that Henry was actually hoping to find the legendary Christian king, Prester John, who was believed to hold court in Africa.

**Prince Henry
the Navigator**

After two years of preparation, the Portuguese fleet attacked Ceuta and had little difficulty in taking the port. A series of mystical portents were said to have marked the journey, amongst which were a solar eclipse and a vision by a monk wherein he saw the Virgin Mary present King Joao with a sword. It was in the port of Ceuta that young Henry first saw the vast wealth of the traders. Spices, precious metals, jewels and fine carpets from the Orient were changing hands at significant profit. We have no doubt that this early experience at Ceuta proved a pivotal point in the life of Prince Henry the Navigator. Five years after the victory at Ceuta, Prince Henry was named the administrator of the Order of Christ, the order's previous master, Dom Lopo Dias de Sousa having died on May 25th of the same year. Prince Henry was only twenty six years of age. Henry's appointment was not thanks to his own merits, but rather at the request of his father, the King of Portugal, who asked the Pope to give the position to his young son. The bull, "In apostolice dignitatis specula" would confirm Henry's status as head of the order. Two years earlier and due to another similar request, Henry's brother was given the helm of the Order of Santiago, which King Dinis had brought under Portuguese rule a century before.

As an administrator of the Order of Christ, Prince Henry had not only manpower at his disposal but also a fleet and the financial resources to finance his explorations of discovery. It is these discoveries for which he is most known, but few are aware of the actual source of the money that financed the trips. Within the first five years of Mastership, Henry and his order were able to colonize the Canaries and Madeira and within another two decades, the Azores. These later profitable expeditions offered Portugal's markets new and exotic goods from Africa, while at the same time filling the coffers of the order to near bursting point. And as this new found wealth continued to grow, so too did the order's power base. In 1456, Pope Calixtus III granted to the order spiritual jurisdiction over all lands from the Capes of Bojador to Guinea and on south to the Indies. This meant that the Grand Prior of the order could levy penalties in these areas.

Prince Henry died on November 13th, 1460 and his son Fernao became the Governor of the order. This leadership would continue in the family until the reign of King Manuel I, who coveted the position for himself. After Henry's son Fernao came Fernao's son, Dom Diogo. Diogo was murdered by King Joao II for trying to overthrow the monarchy. This left the Mastership of the Order of Christ without a logical dynastic heir. The opening was filled by Dom Manuel who would extend his influence from that of Grand Master to King of Portugal in 1495. Manuel sought the Mastery of all three orders; Christ, Santiago and Avis and refused to allow Dom Jorge, the illegitimate son of Joao II to rule the Order of Christ after Manuel had taken the throne for himself. Instead he acted in both capacities, as king of his country and also as master of his order. After twenty one years of relative patience, Manuel eventually came to hold the helm of the remaining two orders. However, by 1492 and the expelling of the last Muslim's from Granada, the military orders began to fail. Despite this, in Portugal the Order of Christ continued to be strong and Manuel I did much to support it, aided by Pope Alexander VI, who issued a bull allowing knights of the order to marry.

At the time of Manuel's coronation there were only 80 commandries, but by the end of his reign in 1521, this number had swelled to 454 commandries spread throughout Portugal, Africa and the Indies. Manuel's successor was King Joao III, who like his predecessor did a great deal to expand the Order of Christ. His reign saw the addition of 990 knights. This expansion may have been more to do with Pope Alexander VI's bull allowing knights of the order to marry than any action taken by King Joao III. The new secularization was popular with the knights and brethren of the order and inspired numerous new recruits to take up the knightly vocation. But reactionary forces existed and in 1530 the Hieronimite priest, Fra Antonio began to reform the order by reinstating the difficult Cistercian rule for the clergy and resumed convent life at Tomar. This drove a wedge between the knights and clerical brethren, to such an extent that many men lost all desire for the life of a Holy Knight of Christ.

The award as it exists today

From the time of Manuel I, the Mastership remained in the hands of the Portuguese Monarchy. During this period the Knights of Christ remained essentially a religious and military order, very similar the order of the Temple that had been its inspiration and mentor. This state of affairs continued up until the reign of Queen Maria, who secularized the order in 1789. This once strong military order, which financed and supported so many new discoveries, ultimately became nothing more important than an order of merit for the Catholic Church.

Today the order is known as 'The Supreme Order of Christ' and as such sits at the top of five Pontifical orders granted by the Holy See. Membership in the 'Supreme Order of Christ' is reserved for Christian heads of state who give evidence of spectacular service. The last time the award of merit was issued was in 1987, when the Pontifical Order was presented to the late Fra Angelo de Mojana, the 77th Grand Master of the Knights of Malta. The award was presented to him to commemorate a quarter century as Master of his order. There are presently no living Knights of Christ, since the last living member, Belgian King Baudin passed away on July 31st, 1993. Since it appears that the Church has no immediate plans to knight new members, it is our conclusion that this particular thread of the Templar web is irrevocably broken. Yet as broken as the Order of Christ would seem to be, those early Portuguese explorations may have led the Templars elsewhere to new lands.

Chapter Six

Templars In America

M uch has been made over the centuries about the wonderful seamanship of the Knights Templar, who in their heyday, sent ships across the length and breadth of the Mediterranean, out into the Atlantic, into the Baltic and the Black sea, and perhaps even around the Continent of Africa. There is also an enduring belief that Templar mariners crossed the Atlantic, and that part of the reason for their great wealth is that they were exploiting silver mines in Central America long before the lure of silver and gold brought the Spaniards to Central and Latin America. Whilst it would be difficult at this time to fully substantiate these claims, there is plenty of evidence from the immediate post-Templar period that even this idea might not be as far fetched as it might at first appear.

Of necessity the Templar Order was extremely secretive about its maritime operations. As the best business people of their day the Templars must have guarded their enterprises carefully. This probably wasn't difficult, because the whole basis of Templar belief and worship seems to have been built upon 'confidentiality ensured by hierarchy'. In other words the more trustworthy one proved to be, the higher up the ladder one climbed, and the more one would get to know. Templar expansion into 'big business' appears to have relied on maintaining the same 'cast-iron' grip on the institution as a whole. Alan's previous research had shown that much of the Templar knowledge ultimately derived from very early European cultures that flourished back as far as the Bronze Age, and that, in the wake of people such as the Minoans, the Mycenaeans and the Phoenicians, it was natural that the Templars should be good sailors. But it is also a fact that many of the Templar Knights were of Norman French ancestry. The Norman's were, essentially, Vikings, who had arrived in France at the start of the Middle Ages (In fact the name 'Norman', is a derivative of 'Norsemen' which in turn means 'The Men of the

North'). It is common knowledge that the Vikings ranged far and wide during their own era, and there are persistent tales, now generally accepted as being true, that the Vikings had visited, and perhaps even placed temporary settlements on, American Soil. Evidence of this is strongest on Canada's east coast, where the first settlement was established on the northernmost peninsula of Newfoundland province at L'Anse aux Meadows. This settlement is believed to date from around 1070 CE. Certainly the post-Templar Henry Sinclair, whose journey to America we shall discuss in due course, was of partly Viking blood, and as Earl of Orkney, he ruled an area of Scotland that had been heavily affected by Viking history. We have dealt, in a previous chapter, with the various theories of the disappearing Templar fleet, a part or all of which could have traveled to the New World. However, since there is no definitive proof that this was the case it has to be admitted that idea of pre 1307 Templar knights standing on American soil must remain, for the present, in the realms of conjecture. But if we have no certain knowledge of the Templars traveling to America prior to their downfall, it is possible to show that in the immediate aftermath of the 1307 persecution, such journeys did take place.

Henry Sinclair, Earl of Orkney embarked for America in May 1398, only a few decades after the Templars were outlawed by the Vatican. Of Henry's Templar ancestry there can be no doubt. The Sinclairs had originally been called St. Clair. Their point of origin was either Pont L'Eveque or St. Clair sur Ept, both of which are in Northern France. Their connection with Templarism extended back to the very start of the Order. Hughes de Payens had been married to a St. Clair heiress, whose family already owned land near to Edinburgh, in Scotland. The very first Templar community outside of France and the Holy Land was at a place south east of Edinburgh which to this day is called 'Temple'. It was built on St. Clair (Sinclair) land and from that point on the Sinclair family was synonymous with the Knights Templar, and latterly with Freemasonry.

Part of the proof of Henry's visit to America is to be found in the foundation of Rosslyn Chapel, not far from Temple and almost immediately south of the Scottish capital. Much has been written about Rosslyn, a curious Gothic structure built during the 15th century, some time after Henry Sinclair's exploits, but still well before the more documented journeys to the Americas, such as the one made by Columbus. As to what Rosslyn Chapel is supposed to be, and why it was built, the reader might be particularly interested in a book entitled 'The Hiram Key' which was written by Christopher Knight and Robert Lomas. They were probably the first authors to point out that amongst the many rich and wonderful carvings to be found within Rosslyn Chapel are any number of representations of both 'Maize heads' and a plant of the 'Aloe cactus' family. Neither of these species were to be found outside of the Americas when Rosslyn was built, and are indigenous to the New World. It would therefore be logical to assume that, at the time Rosslyn Chapel was constructed, no European had ever seen either plant. Earl Henry's journey, and the descriptions he brought back, may well account for the carvings in a building erected by his grandson and it is quite conceivable that this best known Sinclair trip to North America was only one of a number. The journey in question was led by an Italian explorer by the name of Antonio Zeno, who had been employed by Henry Sinclair and the undertaking involved the use of twelve ships. Supposedly the squadron visited what it now Canada and then sailed down the eastern seaboard of the United States. At Westford, Massachusetts, a crude but recognizable tomb stone was found that is said to have been identified as that of 'Sir James Gunn', who died on the voyage. The Gunn's were a Scots clan closely allied to the St. Clair's and the tomb stone is generally accepted as genuine. Meanwhile, in Rosslyn Chapel itself, there is a representation of a single masted ship, with two sails, identical that are shown on the shield of the warrior buried in Massachusetts.

In addition the expedition may well have built a 'round tower' at Newport, Rhode Island, and this has survived. What we found particularly interesting about this tower, is that it bears a striking similarity to both Templar and Scottish architecture. Similar architecture can be found in the Orphir Chapel in Orkney, which was fashioned after the Church of the Holy Sepulcher in Jerusalem. This tower at Rhode Island proves to be an exact copy of the St. Clair church at Corstorphine and it is from this point that Prince Henry St. Clair began his American Journey. The official settlement at Newport was established as late as 1636. However, records from four years previously mentioned the presence of the round tower and had asserted that a European settlement had once existed in the area.

It is highly likely that this voyage, if not actually using

charts already compiled by the Templars, would have created charts of its own, and it is most probably to these that we owe the opening up of America to the frenzy of European exploration that took place at the end of the 15th century and during the decades that followed. It is Alan's belief, as a result of research into other aspects of Templarism, that the Order may well have been in possession of a method of establishing 'longitude' whilst at sea. This knowledge is

Above is the seal of the Knights Templar and to the right is a sketch of the Newport tower bearing a striking similarity.

vital to transoceanic navigation, and Henry's possession of the same information, as a high ranking Templar himself, would have been invaluable to his own American journey. Prince Henry's voyage took place over a century before Columbus embarked on his own epic quest in 1492, by which time the Templars had ceased to exist as a formal institution for nearly two centuries. And yet there are intriguing connections between the journey of Columbus and the Knights Templar.

One of the men who embarked with Earl Henry had the surname Drummond, and it is known that this man's grandson, John Drummond eventually came to live in Madeira. There he became associated with Bartholomew Perstellow, a former Grand Master of the Knights of Christ, and a man whose daughter would eventually marry Christopher Columbus. We have seen that the Knights of Christ, were originally an Iberian branch of the Templar order, who had simply changed names after 1307, under King Dinis I in order to preserve their holdings under Portuguese rule. It was therefore, quite natural that members of the Knights of Christ should keep company with post-Templar Scotsmen of essentially the same persuasion.

Perstellow had known John Drummond's father, and Drummond himself was a friend of Christopher Columbus. It is therefore most likely that Columbus possessed charts pertaining to Henry Sinclair's own trip to America, as well as maps that might have belonged to his father in law. The former is certainly true for John Drummond was called before the Spanish Queen Isabella to swear as to the genuine nature of Columbus' maps. All three of the ships commanded by Columbus carried red Templar crosses on their sails and there can, in total, be little doubt that Templar knowledge funded the enterprise. It is now accepted in many circles that Christopher Columbus himself may well have been a member of the Order of the Knights of Christ. This would seem to be largely due to the fact that his father-in-law was a member of the brotherhood.

A less well known mariner of the same period as Columbus was John Cabot. Cabot was born in Italy and had led a quite breathtaking life, though his most famous journeys were undertaken beneath an English flag. Under the patronage of Henry VII of England, John Cabot set sail in 1497 and by midsummer's day, June 24th, he was wading ashore in Newfoundland. There are important facts relating to John Cabot that merit closer scrutiny in Templar terms. First there is the nature of the man. It is known, for example, that Cabot was one of the first Europeans to ever visit the sacred Muslim site of Mecca. It will be recalled by most readers that the Templars had a particular fascination for the Muslim religion, an interest that was obviously shared by Cabot and expressed in a 'singular' and potentially dangerous fashion.

Cabot's point of departure is also interesting because he chose the port of Bristol, on the west coast of England. Bristol owes its very existence to the Templars, who had the free exportation of wool from Bristol to La Rochelle during the reign of Henry III of England. For this reason, Bristol marked the site of one of the Templars most important British foundations and ports. The idea that the Americas were unknown at Cabot's time is dismissed immediately in the knowledge that fishing fleets were regularly catching huge amounts of Cod off the Banks of Newfoundland, long before Cabot even arrived in the port. The knowledge of North American waters possessed by some of Cabot's crew, signed on as they were in Bristol, would have been invaluable. If none of these facts particularly sets John Cabot apart as being a post-Templar sympathizer, then the date of his arrival in Newfoundland probably does. His chosen day of disembarkation was the feast of St. John the Baptist. This was a saint for whom the Templars had displayed a constant devotion. Cabot chose the name 'St. John's' for his first settlement, and this was to become the capital city of Newfoundland. In fact although Christopher Columbus undertook his voyage somewhat earlier than John Cabot, Cabot has the better claim to America, since Columbus only got as far as Cuba. Bearing all the known information in mind it is highly likely that Cabot's voyage also relied heavily on maps created during the Templar era.

Cabot sought to strengthen his position with regard to his discoveries by commanding a later and much larger expedition. During this second visit to the Americas his ships disappeared, though this does not necessarily mean that they were lost. Some years later, but still thirteen years before any Spaniard set foot on the American mainland, the Spanish cartographer, Juan de la Cosa produced a map detailing the eastern coast of the American Continent. This map clearly showed the places that De la Cosa firmly believed had been visited, and settled by, British navigators. These may well have been part of the legacy of Cabot's second voyage, though why he so effectively disappeared from English and European history remains a mystery.

Even if John Cabot's fleet foundered before making a second landfall in America, De la Cosa's English flags may represent the much earlier efforts of Sinclair's expedition.

There is an interesting footnote to this story because when the Pilgrim Fathers, aboard the Mayflower, arrived in Massachusetts America, on the 4th of December, 1640, they appeared to know very well where they wanted to disembark, even though it has been generally assumed that they had been blown off course from an intended Virginia colony. Alan has shown, in his book 'The Rose and the Grail,' that the Lieden Brotherhood, which had financed the Mayflower expedition, certainly had Rosicrucian and possibly post-

Templar connections. Within a day or two of coming ashore the Pilgrim Father's had discovered the remnants of a European settlement slightly inland from Cape Cod. It had been either destroyed or abandoned at some earlier date but that, with the whole virgin North American seaboard to explore, the Mayflower pilgrims should happen across a European colony, albeit abandoned, by accident, is stretching credibility too far. In fact this might well have been one of the settlements shown on De la Cosa's map, or on a Templar chart of an earlier date.

Another interesting early character, and one roughly contemporary with Henry Sinclair was Henry the Navigator, son of Joao I of Portugal, who's connection to the Templars and the latter Order of Christ, we looked at last chapter. Prince Henry's contribution to exploration did not lay in commanding his own vessel, because he rarely if ever did so. Henry the Navigator simply used the wealth of his beloved order and his own expertise to assist other seaman, and by so doing amassed himself a great fortune. Being Governor of the Knights of Christ, Henry too had access to Templar maps and charts, and though it is not recorded that he ever sponsored an expedition to the New World, his patrons were active in most of the known seas and oceans of his time. His efforts represented a continuation of the great mercantile efforts of the Templars, and even if he did not choose to acquaint himself with America, it is highly likely that he associated himself with others who did.

And so it can be seen, in the details of these early voyages to the Americas that the Knights Templar, whilst still a legal and recognized body, almost certainly gained and retained knowledge of the physical reality of the New World. Future research may throw more light upon pre 1307 Templar settlements or mercantile ventures in the Americas. Of the post-Templar idealism rooted in the Rosicrucian movement, and within Freemasonry, and of the part this played in the establishment of the United States of America, there can be no doubt. It is now becoming increasingly obvious that the very fabric of the United States of America was founded on the philosophical, religious and even the economic ideals that Templarism brought to Europe from the 12th century on.

Chapter Seven

The Rose Cross

Few symbols are less understood today than that of the Rose Cross. As a modern movement Rosicrucianism may have little to say about its antecedents and even the symbol itself is misunderstood. It is generally accepted that 'Rose Cross' alludes to a cross that is 'pink' in color, in deference to the French 'rose', which retains that linguistic meaning. But though the Rose Cross may be nowhere near as old as some previous authorities claim it to be, it can still be traced back to the period during the 11th century, when the Crusaders held much of the Holy Land for Christianity. Templar graves have been found in several sites in Palestine which contain a carved effigy of a warrior's sword, which itself is a cruciform shape, around which are entwined roses. If these tomb covers were ever colored, they certainly are not today, but they bear testimony to the fact that the Rose Cross was originally nothing to do with the color of the motif, but with the flower that entwines the cross.

It is possible that this connection alone is enough to indicate that there is some tangible connection between a strange religious movement that appeared in Europe in the early 17th century, and those Templars who fell to sickness or the sword in the Holy Land several centuries earlier.

The rose flower is alive with mystery and folklore, and has long been associated with the part that the 'feminine' plays in religion. It is not the province of this book to explore such matters in detail and interested readers might care to delve deeper by looking at Alan's research in his book "The Rose and the Grail." However, it is probably necessary to point out that the route taken by the rose into Templar beliefs probably owes a great deal to a pre-Christian deity called 'Rosemerth', who was worshiped in Lorraine (now part of France) since time out of hand. It was at her shrine, Sion Vaudemont, that the Virgin Mary was first named 'Queen of Heaven', a theme which St. Bernard of Clairvaux took up some 60 years later. St.

Bernard influenced the Vatican to offer Mary this position officially, and the roses of Rosemerth have surrounded the Virgin ever since.

However, there is a fascinating sequel to this story since, as a botanist friend recently revealed, the common European Dog Rose (Rosa Caninis) is rare amongst plants in that it does not have to be cross fertilized to produce its fruit, the rosehip. In this sense the rose is capable of virgin birth, and it seems unlikely that this potential was lost on our distant ancestors.

If it was our intention to fully explore the extraordinary symbolism of this flower, the connections between roses and the Catholic faith alone would require a chapter of their own. However, we hope the reader will be happy to accept our assurance that St. Bernard and his family members associated the rose with the Virgin Mary. The earliest patron of the Knights Templar was the Virgin Mary, and St. Bernard of Clairvaux was deeply involved in the formation of the order, so it is not surprising that Templar graves initiated the idea of the 'Rose Cross'.

Many fascinating, but almost certainly comparatively modern, stories, connect the Rose Cross with ancient Egyptian deities and once again we direct the interested reader to Alan's "The Grail and the Rose." For our purposes the first time that the Rose Cross was mentioned in conjunction with a contemporary and espoused religious belief was in the early part of the 17th century, when a series of documents known as the 'Rosicrucian Manifestoes' began to circulate in Western Europe. Authorship of these documents has never been irrefutably established, but they were probably written by a man called Johann Valentin Andrea a Protestant preacher from Württemburg in Germany. At this period Europe was being deeply damaged by the Thirty Years War, which represented the death knell of Catholicism as the driving religious and political force in Western Europe. For a while the Catholic forces made great gains and Protestant sympathizers flocked out of Europe, and especially Holland, to find refuge in England. Many of them were aided in their flight by a Masonic type institution known as 'The Christian Unions'. The main organizer of these clandestine brotherhoods was Andrea, also supposedly author of the Rosicrucian Manifestoes.

From the start Rosicrucianism proclaimed for itself an ancient pedigree, and the published material gives more than one hint that the movement equated itself with Templar ideals, even though it was fervently Protestant, whereas the Templars had at least espoused an enduring service of the Mother Church of Rome. But such a connection might not be so surprising as it appears. The very Catholic Church which the Templars had sworn to protect, in the form of Pope Clement V, had conspired to destroy the whole Templar order at a stroke. This must have seemed like treachery of the most base sort and may have been enough to drive post Templar sympathizers into the hands of the reformed Church.

We must also bear in mind that Protestantism owes its survival to the city of Geneva, where it was carefully nurtured by Calvin. The relevance of this fact will become obvious in a later section of our book. Following the first two Rosicrucian Manifestoes, there followed, in 1616 what we consider to be one of the most intriguing documents ever to surface in Europe. It is called 'The Chymical Wedding of Christian Rozenkreutz'. This document is essentially a story relating to the adventures of Christian Rozenkreutz when he is invited to a 'magical wedding' of a king and queen in a mysterious land.

The story is couched in alchemical symbolism and typifies the ideals and thoughts of many learned people in Europe at the time, not least of all Englishmen such as Francis Bacon. Alchemy was a popular study and owed little to our present conception that it existed merely to turn base metals into gold. In fact the true search of the alchemist was a sort of spiritual enlightenment that lay at the heart of the 'Utopian' ideals of whoever wrote "The Chymical Wedding." Christian, the hero of the story, is a kind of humble magician, and there is no doubt that moral imperatives lay at the heart of the work. But what is even more interesting in our terms is the fact that the book has all the hall marks of the much earlier 'Holy Grail' stories.

The Holy Grail became popular at the end of the Crusades and though it came to be associated with the cup from which Christ drank at the Last Supper, its origins lay lost in the mists of prehistory, as a sacred cauldron. It is interesting to realize that the very first Grail Story, written by Cretien de Troyes, in about 1188, was produced in the very city where Templarism was born. Subsequent Grail stories emanated from various parts of Europe, and many of them mentioned Templar, or Templar type knights, and espoused their virtues as peerless and Holy knights. It is more than probable that, from first to last, Templars, or post-Templars either wrote or sanctioned many of the Grail stories.

The Chymical Wedding of Christian Rozenkreutz seems to be the Holy Grail brought up to date. Once again, it does not specifically mention Templars, but the same values espoused by the Grail cycles is in evidence at every stage. Rosicrucianism certainly recognized its own link with Templarism, and it is a connection which we do not doubt for a moment.

The Rosicrucians believed that all people should be free, and that they could establish their own union with the Godhead, through self purification and a search for the 'source' of everything. They believed absolutely in personal responsibility but, although the very name of the hero of the Chymical Wedding is Christian, if this fact is meant to be taken at face value and is not a deliberate pun on the part of the writer, then his Christianity was of a very different sort which would have damned Rosicrucianism to perdition. In fact there is nothing overtly Christian about The Chymical Wedding, which smacks at a reverence for the old 'Mystery' religions of Europe, together with a philosophical rationalism that the Church of the day would never have condoned.

Nobody is really sure where Rosicrucianism developed, but if it was in the Germany of Andrea, then it arose in a place where Templarism had managed to survive almost intact. The Teutonic Knights, an early offshoot of the Templars, undoubtedly took runaway Templars back into its own fold after 1307 and in any case no prosecutions were held in what is now Germany, partly because the authorities were terrified of the Knights Templar. In addition Württemburg is extremely close to the Swiss border, which once again should become relevant in the later stages of this book.

Whatever its source, and no matter what its true ancestry, Rosicrucianism hit the spot as far as many Europeans of the early 17th century were concerned. It appeared to have much in common with Freemasonry, and is held as a Masonic degree these days. This triple connection of Templarism, Rosicrucianism and Freemasonry proved to be a heady mixture and one that had much to do with the eventually free government of the United States of America.

Rosicrucian ideals grew apace, and nowhere more so than in Britain, though it is impossible to assert that such ideas were anything out of the ordinary to a particular section of society in Britain at the time. A particular group of early Freemasons, most of whom also enjoyed Rosicrucian leanings, had already formed themselves, by the start of the 17th century, into a fraternity called 'The Invisible College'. It was the avowed intention of these people to rediscover ancient truths and to allow learning in science to flourish without the restrictive influence of religious authorities being allowed to stifle knowledge. These people were eventually to form the Royal Society and some of its earliest members, people such as Newton, Boyle and Wren became household names.

Most of the first members of the Royal Society were either known Rosicrucians, or else were staunch supporters of similar ideals. The list of Freemasons who also espoused Rosicrucian ideals even includes men such as George Washington, Benjamin Franklin and numerous other individuals who saw service in the American War of Independence and who went on to found a country, the constitution of which, is replete with Rosicrucian statements and sentiments.

Templarism survived in a host of different forms in the long, dark years after the treacherous attempt of Philip le Bel to eradicate the order at a stroke. Whilst religious soldiers down in far off Portugal were still wearing the pattee cross of the Knights of Christ and were still espousing strictly Catholic beliefs, the ex Templars further north had taken a different approach to their survival. By the time of the Rosicrucian Manifestoes there can surely have been no connection between such apparently diverse groupings, though each, in its own way, had been originally inspired by a common heritage.

It is extremely doubtful if the first stirrings of rebellion against the Catholic Church, again propagated by a German, Martin Luther, of the 16th century, could ever have become the raging force for reform that it proved to be in the following century, without the bravery and persistence of men and women who held Rosicrucian ideals. It was their notion of a state free from corruption, greed and destructive dogma that allowed the cry for freedom to begin echoing around Western Europe and which also tempted liberty seeking Europeans to brave the chill waters of the Atlantic.

In the case of the latter it had been the survival of Templar seamanship, maps and charts, and the efforts of Templar inspired explorers that had opened up the New World to their Utopian dreams. The Templar knights could conceivably have been the first Europeans to found settlements on the mainland of North America and so the hard won freedoms of the first citizens of the United States of America were ultimately built on Templar foundations from not one, but several different sources.

Chapter Eight

The Passing Of The Torch

N o discussion of the survival of the Knights Templar would be complete without the inclusion of a document discovered in the early nineteenth century and said to date back to the early fourteenth century. If this were a document detailing some apparently insignificant aspect of Templar history, we would not include it in the body of this book, but since this document in question discloses, or seemingly so, the complete line of survival of the Templars from the arrest in 1307 to its existence in modern times, we feel it is not only pertinent to the discussion, but rather essential.

The document to which we refer is known as the "Carta Transmissionis" or Charter of transmission and it purports to be a list of all the Grand Masters of the order from De Molay to modern times. The reader will no doubt ask the immediate question, "Is the document authentic?" A fair question, and one that we will attempt to answer in due course. However, we feel emboldened to point out that history is as authentic as the beliefs of those who wrote it. The Emperor Napoleon once said, "What is history, but a fable agreed upon?" and as we will see in the case of the Larmenius charter, which was named for the first alleged Grand Master of the Templars following De Molay, this possible fable has been agreed upon by at least one Neo-Templar order, "The Sovereign Military Order of the Templar of Jerusalem" or "SMOTJ."

Not wishing to move too far ahead of ourselves, we will step back to the period of history where the document in question was discovered. The period of the French Revolution was a turbulent one ending in the death of the French King. The dynasty which ended with Louis, at the guillotine, was seen by some as a logical extension of the same French crown that destroyed the Templar order, some four centuries earlier. It is during Louis' execution that someone in the crowd is said to have jumped onto the scaffold, dipped his fingers into the monarch's fallen blood and yelled out, "Jacques De Molay you are avenged." This unknown individual then disappeared into the crowd. Now if this story is to be taken at face value, and we certainly have no cause to believe otherwise, it proves that to at least some notion, Templarism was still very much alive in the minds of certain French people in the 18th century.

We both agree that Freemasonry commenced far earlier than the standard recognized date of 1717, nevertheless it is from this date that historians recognize the Craft. In fact it had grown rapidly in term of lodges and Masons in the short span of eighty years prior to the French Revolution. By this time the notion of the Chivalric (knightly) degrees had begun to arise, largely due to the 1736 lecture of Andrew Michael Ramsay, a Scottish Freemason living in France, who claimed that the Masonic Order had actually began in Jerusalem during the First Crusade, with the religious fighting orders. It is important to note for future reference that although Ramsay is accredited with being the first person to link the Masons to the former Templars, nowhere in his oration is the term Knights Templar given. With this speech, nonetheless the Masonic Lodges began to introduce rituals revolving around both the Knights Templar and the rival Hospitalers.

It was the German, Baron Karl Von Hundt, who in 1754, made the connection between the Freemasons and the Knights Templar in which he contended the former was a direct descendent of the latter. His degrees of Freemasonry became known as the "Rite of Strict Observance" and Strict Observance Lodges still exist to this day. Von Hundt claimed that the doomed Jacques De Molay passed the Master's torch to one Pierre d'Aumont, who Von Hundt claimed was the Preceptor of Auvergne. D'Aumont is said to have fled with two commanders and five brother knights to the island of Mull off the coast of Scotland where, disguised as Operative Masons, they later went on to form Freemasonry as a continuation of the order of the Temple.

It appears there are a couple of problems with Von Hundt's line of continuation. Firstly, the Preceptor of Auvergne who was arrested in England was actually, Imbert Blanke. Secondly, as pointed out by the authors Baigent and Leigh, the island of Mull was owned by Edward II, a staunch enemy of King Robert the Bruce of Scotland and himself instructed to persecute the Templars, so this was a highly unlikely place for a group of French Templars to flee.

As false as Von Hundt's claims may have been, the Rite of Strict Observance continued to grow in popularity among the Freemasons of the time and Templar degrees were popular among the Craft. Of course some Freemasons did not readily accept that the order descended from the crusading Templars. This is probably because, at the time, the general populace still contended that the Templars were guilty of the accusations that had brought them down over four hundred years earlier. Such public opinions were fed by the popular author Sir Walter Scott, himself a Freemason, who painted a grim picture of the Templar knights in both "Ivanhoe" and "The Talisman." There were even some Freemasons of this time that truly believed that the Templar/Freemason connection was a plot put forth by the Catholic Jesuit order to damage the Freemasons. Old habits die hard and the same sort of action continues to this day perpetuated by the fundamentalist Christian sect, which Stephen covered thoroughly in his book, "Unholy Worship."

It was shortly after the turn of the 19th century that Templarism would meet with its greatest resurgence, perhaps due to the ground work set forth by the Masonic degrees and the ideas put forth by Von Hundt and his predecessor Ramsay. In 1804, a Dr. Bernard Raymond Fabre Palaprat, claimed to have discovered the document mentioned earlier in the chapter. Palaprat asserted that he had found not only the Charter of Transmission of Larmenius, but also 27 pages of documentation which were dated to 1705 and said to be the statutes of the surviving Templar order.

Palaprat's story was that in 1792, Louis-Hercule Timoleon, the Duc de Cosse Brissac, the last "Secret" Grand Master of the Knights Templar, being in fear of his life and facing execution, strove to ensure the continuation of the order. He is alleged to have passed on the Templar torch to a brother named Claude-Mathieu Radix de Chavillon, who in 1804 turned down the Grand Master's chair in favor of Fabre Palaprat, who, as a result, became the highest ranking officer of the new public Order of the Temple.

This transmission of powers was granted by the document know as the "Carta Transmissionis", which was allegedly the passing of the Templar Mastership from Jacques De Molay to John Mark Larmenius in 1314, who continued the order in secrecy; in turn giving way to Thomas Theobald of Alexandria and so on down the line of time to the French Revolution, after which the order went public. The list of suggested Grand Masters is as follows:

Alleged List Of Grand Masters 1313-1804

1313-1324	John-Marc Larmenius
1324-1340	Thomas Theobald of Alexandria
1340-1349	Arnaud de Braque
1349-1357	Jean de Claremont
1357-1381	Bertrand du Guesclin
1381-1392	Bernard Arminiacus
1419-1451	Jean Arminiacus
1451-1472	Jean de Croy
1472-1478	Bernard Imbault
1478-1497	Robert Leononcourt
1497-1516	Galeatius de Salazar
1516-1544	Phillippe Chabot
1544-1574	Gaspard de Galtiaco Tavanensis
1574-1615	Henri de Montmorency
1615-1651	Charles de Valois
1651–1681	Jacques Ruxellius de Granceio
1681-1705	Jacques Henri Duc de Duras
1705-1724	Phillippe, Duc d'Orleans
1724-1737	Louis Augustus Bourbon
1737-1741	Louis Henri Bourbon Conde
1741-1776	Louis-Francois Boubon Conti
1776-1792	Louis-Hercule Timoleon, Duc de Cosse Brissac
1792-1804	Claude-Mathieu Radix de Chavillon
1804-1838	Bernard Raymond Fabre Palaprat (discovered list)

The document, claimed by Palaprat to date to the year 1324, is argued by some to be a forgery. The assertions suggesting a fraud include the fact that, although the document is written in Latin as one would expect a document of that period to be, the Latin used is a more modern version of the language and therefore points rather suspiciously to a more contemporary origin. Additionally the signatures of successive Grand Masters, said to be written in their own blood, holds a clue for those who would claim the document to be a hoax. The alleged Grand Master from 1357-1381, Bertrand du Guesclin, whose name is clearly included on the document, was illiterate and therefore could not have signed his name with anything other than an "X". However, since even illiterate individuals often learn at least how to construct a signature, we remain open minded on this particular point. In any case the supporters of the document claim that De Guesclin's name was written by one of the Brethren in order to cover up the ignorance of the Grand Master.

Whether this document was an authentic treasure of Templar history or a blatant forgery by Fabre Palaprat, it is nonetheless accepted by as many as it is disputed by others. With our previous research and discussion on the possibility of Templars fleeing to Scotland, the reader may be interested in a portion of the Larmenius documents that refer to these Scottish brethren as deserters and traitors to the order:

"Lastly, with the decree of the Grand Convent of the Brethren, by my supreme delegated authority, I will, declare, and decree the Scotch Templars "deserters of the Order, cast off with an anathema, they and their brethren of St. John of Jerusalem, despoilers of the dominions of the Militia (to whom may God show mercy), without the pale of the Temple, now and for ever. "

What we find most interesting about this passage, whether deemed a forgery or not, is the acceptance of the reality of the Scottish Templars. If this is an authentic document then it proves that the Scottish Templars did exist and were condemned by the order. If a forgery it shows that Palaprat or whoever wrote the document, probably accepted their existence as a Templar continuation and did not relish the competition for his new or revitalized order.

To add to the authenticity of the Larmenius Charter and to lend support to the newfound order, Palaprat retained his own form of Holy Relics. He is said to have purchased a copper reliquary which contained among other things, several documents affixed with official looking seals and a sword purported to be the sword of the last non secret Grand Master, Jacques de Molay. It was one item of a more morbid nature that was the finishing touch to create the air of authenticity. These were some charred bones wrapped in linen cloth, said to be the bones of the martyred Grand Master himself.

With everything in place, a large ceremony was held at the Church of St. Paul in Paris, in 1808, where Jacques De Molay was honored together with various other martyrs of the order. The ceremony itself took on a very official form with Fabre Palaprat, as Grand Master dressed in the regalia of his new found office; there was even a detachment of French infantry lining the aisle creating a very impressive show for the French people. During the Funeral orations, rumors are said to have circulated through the throngs of people that Napoleon himself protected this order. This contention was made bearing in mind his difficult relationship with the Catholic Church. The order of SMOTJ to this day contends that Napoleon indeed did support the order giving it official recognition as the restored order of the Templars. If this is the case, one can not avoid wondering whether this bore testimony to Napoleon's belief that the order truly descended from Hughes de Payens or on account of his own Masonic affiliations? It is generally accepted by historians that one had to be first a Freemason to belong to Palaprat's order of the Temple, so the support of Napoleon certainly does have some merit in terms of being a plausible theory. This Masonic affiliation continued up until the year 1811. It was also in this year that Palaprat would rewrite the statutes supposedly set down in 1705, thus causing the first of many schisms that would face the order in years to come. It was almost as if, as we will soon learn, Palaprat was setting in motion the actions that would mature 19 years later.

Around 1830, Palaprat, arguably the luckiest man in history when it came to finding hidden and secret documents, made another 'discovery' of vital Templar importance. In a book shop on the Seine, he claimed to have come upon a manuscript, written in Greek called, "The Leviticon."

This document, he believed, held the true beliefs of the Knights Templar and that those beliefs were of a Johannite and possibly a Gnostic orientation. Since the Johannite belief system would play an important part in the story of the Order of the Temple, a few words should be said to describe its tenets for those who are unfamiliar with the concepts.

Gnostic is a word often confused with agnostic, who doubt or are unsure of the existence of God. the word Gnostic comes from the Greek, "Gnosis" which means "to know", therefore Agnostic is aptly explained as "not knowing." It is believed that the Cathars, who were persecuted by the Church in Southern France during the Albigensian Crusade practiced a Gnostic belief system, which held that theirs was the true Christianity.

The Johannite beliefs are similar in nature and revolve around the figure of St. John the Baptist, who was an important saint to the Templar Knights. The feast of St. John, June 24th, was instructed to be observed by the Templars very Rule of Order. The battle of Bannockburn and the landing of John Cabot in Canada both occurred on the date of June 24th and the Grand Lodge of England was formed on June 24th, 1717, thus implying connections to the Templar order.

These days we tend to see the image of John the Baptist as that written in the Gospels of the New Testament, but to many the interpretation and veneration of John the Baptist is of a different import. To the Sabeans and Mandaeans, John was regarded as the true prophet rather than Jesus. These same groups regarded Jesus as a heretic and rebel who deceived men and perverted the teachings of John the Baptist. The Mandaeans further believed that Jerusalem was created by Ru Ha, a powerful and evil Goddess. This Goddess worked evil through several human agencies, these being Abraham, Moses, David, Solomon and lastly Jesus. Jesus in turn, according to the Mandaean Johannite beliefs, was baptized by John the Baptist and learned many truths from him. These teachings of John were not propounded by Jesus and instead, they assert, he taught people different lessons and led them astray. The Johannites believed that after the death of John and with the corrupt teachings of Jesus the world fell to a horrible error.

Some supposed aspects of Johannite belief are said to be based on the "Toladat Yoshu", a Talmudic text. In this account of the life of Jesus, he was seen as the illegitimate son of Miriam (Mary) who was made pregnant by a Roman soldier named Pandera. In this account Miriam takes the child Jesus to Egypt where he is initiated into the Osirian mysteries. To this sect of Johannites, the concept of God, viewed as "existence, action and mind" is very reminiscent of Easter mysticism of the 'Zen' variety. True, this is definitely a trinity of a sort but very different to that of 'the Father, the Son and the Holy Ghost,' venerated by the Church of Rome. It is to this trinity that Palaprat, with his Leviticon, professed to be at the heart of the true doctrine of the Knights Templar.

This doctrine, which Palaprat refereed to as 'the Primitive Christian Church' was, he suggested, handed down from St. John, through the Jewish patriarchs to Theoclet, who was sixtieth in a line of succession. He in turn passed this sacred knowledge to Hughes de Payens who in turn carried it through the Templar Masters, overt and covert, to wind up in Palaprat's hands. We cannot avoid remarking, perhaps flippantly, how lucky Fabre was to discover this extremely important document on a Paris bookstall.

With his new found spirituality and Johannite convictions, Palaprat tried to instill the newfound knowledge into a few brethren, who seemingly showed no interest. Palaprat, by this stage, near mad with the zeal of his faith, sought the assistance of a defrocked Catholic Priest named Father Chatel. In a rather elaborate ceremony in Montmartre, Palaprat was made a Bishop in the Johannite faith and was awarded the title, "Primate of the Gauls." With his new Ecclesiastic power, Fabre Palaprat, began to enforce the Johannite beliefs on the order of the Temple. The resistance of the Templar brothers resulted in the second schism in the two decades of his Mastership of the order.

Palaprat fell ill in 1837 which gave the order an opportunity to make alterations. His death one year later, in February, 1838 allowed, not only for his removal, but also that of his imposed Johannite beliefs. The order immediately called a 'convent general' and due to the corruption of their original 1705 statutes by Palaprat rewrote them all, removing any trace of the Johannite practices of the previous Grand Master and restoring their allegiances to the Catholic faith and the Holy See. It is our contention that the current Order of the Temple, the SMOTJ, would prefer all Johannite connections to conveniently disappear. We reach this conclusion in the face of a complete denial by those to whom we spoke, of any knowledge that the Johannite practices were once part of the organization's statutes. But in fairness to the modern representatives of the order, it is just conceivable that this may be as a result of a lack of knowledge of the order's history, rather than any attempt to divert our research.

The next Grand Master of the order was the English Admiral, Sir William Sidney Smith. Smith was introduced into the order while on a mission to Cyprus, and is mentioned by his biographer, John Barrow. According to Barrow, Sir William landed at Cyprus in 1799 and was able to quash an insurrection of Jannisaries. After his victory the Admiral visited the Greek Archbishop in Nicosia, who presented Sidney-Smith with the

Templar Cross, which the Archbishop wore as an emblem of his
Episcopal office. This very same emblem was said to belong to
Richard I who received it during the Crusades. Sidney-Smith was
then made a knight of the order and given the position of Grand Prior
of England. After the death of Palaprat, he was awarded the highest
honor, that of Grand Master.

It would prove to be an honor that met with disfavor among
the French brethren who refused to accept an Englishman at the helm
of their order. This resulted in the order's third schism and the French
knights began to select their own leaders. It was because of the
upheaval in France that many of the European branches of the order
became autonomous. Sir William Sidney-Smith died in 1840, just
two years after taking the reins from the apparently mad Palaprat.

From the period of Smith's death to the turn of the twentieth
century, the order both expanded and continued to suffer from
schism's. The year 1845 saw the Prince de Chimay seek the
assistance of Pope Gregory XVI in reversing the ban laid down by
the bull of Clement V, declaring the Templars disbanded and heretic.
Gregory did concede to a certain extent declaring that all modern
Templars must be Roman Catholics. Whether by approaching the
Vatican the order simply sought to gain papal favor or if it wished to
rid itself once and for all the Johannite tendencies once put forth by
Palaprat, we cannot judge. However, it should be noted that the
proposed Catholicism did not meet with the approval of all members
of the order and in 1865, the Belgium Priory split, forming the Priory
of St. John for the Catholics and the Priory of the Trinity of the
Tower for others. Perhaps this demonstrates that the Johannite beliefs
were not quite dead. The latter Priory adopted the Strict Observance
Freemasonry degrees created by Baron Von Hundt, which we
discussed earlier in the chapter. The Catholic Chapter would prove
to be the shortest lived, falling by the wayside only a quarter of a
century later in 1890. The Trinity Tower Priory survived through the
new century coming to a end with its last meeting in 1930.

Two years later the order adopted the name which it holds
to this day. In that year nine Templars, obviously emblematic of the
original nine knight founders of 1118, held a chapter in Belgium
wherein a Grand Prior was chosen along with the name, "The
Sovereign Military Order of the Temple of Jerusalem." One of the
first Priories to join the newly reestablished order was the Priory of

Switzerland, which as we will see later in this chapter was very powerful within the Templar order.

Ten years later during the Second World War, the Belgium Templar Master, Vandencourt, fearing Nazi persecution, transferred all documents to the protection of the Portuguese Grand Prior, Antonio Campello De Sousa Fontes. At the end of the war, De Sousa Fontes refused to return the documents to the Belgium Priory. Vandencourt died shortly after due to a tragic accident, at which time De Sousa Fontes decided to seize the Templar throne as Grand Regent of the order. This assumption of the chair was undertaken without the consent of the order and resulted in yet another schism, which we conclude seem to have permeated to the very soul of Palaprat's invention. Three years after taking the Templar helm De Sousa Fonte declared his son Fernando 'heir apparent' of the order and twelve years later on the death of De Sousa, Fernando was named Grand Regent of the SMOTJ.

The Sovereign Military Order of the Temple of Jerusalem had grown to a large number of Priories scattered throughout the continent of Europe and the Mediterranean as well as south America, but this did not take account of the United States of America. This fell under the jurisdiction of the aforementioned Priory of Switzerland, one of the first Priories in the order.

It seems that during the 1960's there were a considerable number of SMOTJ, Templars of Swiss descent living in the United states. At the request of Anton Leuprecht, who was not only the Grand Master of Switzerland but also the Mondial Chief of all Autonomous Grand Priories of the world, a number of Americans were invited to join. A meeting was held on March 31st, 1962 in Verona, New jersey at the home of William Pryor, where the ground work was laid down forming the Autonomous Grand Priory of the United States. This was confirmed in a letter of April 16th, 1962 from the Grand Prior of Switzerland, Anton Leuprecht. What remains of particular interest to us on account of our own research and theories of Templar continuance is the degree of importance placed on Switzerland in forming and sanctioning the American Grand Priory. It remains to be seen whether Leuprecht was acting largely on behalf of the Autonomous Swiss Priory or as his status as Chief of all autonomous Priories world wide.

The 1970's saw a change in hands of the Mastership, since

many of the Grand Priors did not accept the De Sousa heir as a proper candidate for his office, even though he had already held the position for ten years. At a General Chapter held in France, Antoine Zdrojewski was elected as the orders Grand Master. In 1973, the new Grand Master declared each Grand Priory autonomous and it has remained this way to the present time.

Today the order has autonomous Grand Priories spread out around the globe and is once again a Christian organization, although that restriction no longer requires a specifically Catholic faith. In the words of the orders own informational booklet:

"Therefore the Order is truly international and is Ecumenical, as the order does not restrict membership to any single Christian Denomination. The Order is not part of any Masonic cabal, does not engage in politics and does not encourage or allow members to act contrary to their obligations to their country."

What remains today is an order that appears to be descended from those nine knights who formed a bond of protection and service to the memory of the Temple for which they were named in 1118. The Sovereign Military Order of the Temple of Jerusalem stands as an order that serves those same ideals set down in the Levant eight centuries ago. Is all of this to be accepted as historical fact, or is it based on a mutually acceptable fable? And should we view the Larmenius Charter as an historically authentic document, or the forgery of a French Megalomaniac with Johannite tendencies? The whole topic is so serfused with speculation that we must leave the final answer of this question to the integrity and consideration of you, our reader.

Chapter Nine

The Temple And Freemasonry

In the last chapter it will have become obvious to the reader that, at least during the last two centuries or so, there have been groups of individuals who on the one hand declared themselves to Freemasons, and who, on the other, claimed a lineal descent from the Knights Templar. Before examining the possibility of this belief we must first state the generally recognized facts concerning Freemasonry. According to Grand Lodge in London, Freemasonry began in 1717, with the formation of Grand Lodge, whereas the Knights Templar were disbanded and dissolved not so long after the 1307 persecutions of King Philip IV of France. It follows therefore that there was a gap of four full centuries between the last Templar and the first Freemason. However, life is hardly ever straight forward, and any person who has looked at the issues carefully must first come to the conclusion that not only did the Knights Templar, in one form or another, very definitely survive beyond 1307, but that Freemasonry, in one form or another, significantly predates the 18th century.

Freemasons do not consist of one cohesive body, centrally run and all encompassing. The Masonic fraternity consists of the individual members who gather in individual lodges. These lodges are in turn governed by a Grand Lodge. Although each Grand Lodge world wide recognizes each other, there is no one universal governing jurisdiction. With this in mind it becomes obvious that Grand Lodge, London, cannot speak for all those men who form themselves into fraternal groups that they, themselves, refer to as Freemasonry. In any case the idea would be absurd, for it is a proven fact that there were Masonic institutions, not only in Scotland but also in England, for a considerable period prior to 1717. Killwinning Lodge in Scotland approached Grand Lodge for recognition as the oldest Scottish Lodge. The Grand Lodge refused and Killwinning removed itself from the Grand Lodge and formed its own Lodge.

They formed many lodges carrying the Killwinning name and one exists to this day in the United States. Killwinning later rejoined the Grand Lodge family.

The situation is complicated because Freemasonry, even of the Grand Lodge variety, claims for itself a truly ancient history, which encompasses Egyptian, Mesopotamian and Greek components, with a heavy bias placed on the area around Jerusalem at the time of King Solomon. To the outsider this sounds rather like a cultural cook, walking in the herb garden of history and taking a leaf here and a stalk there, as he sees fit, in order to create a meal that would give the true researcher into the past intellectual indigestion. However, the majority of Masons would say that it is the worth of the fraternity today that really counts, irrespective of the validity of its claims of ancient lineage.

Masonic Knight Templar circa 1800's

The only fair yardstick to use in judging the genuine origination of 'the Craft' would be that supplied by known facts. If we can find hard historical evidence, then we can compare that evidence with what Freemasonry thinks about itself. We may then have reached the truth. But we can at least commence with a paradigm, if only to tell us where to start our inquiry. And an enduring paradigm of many branches of Freemasonry is that they owe their very existence to Templarism.

Not only does the fraternity owe its existence to Templarism, the fraternity seems to loudly proclaim it in a number of ways. As we will see later in this chapter, the Masonic body known as the York Rite contains three sub groups called, The Royal Arch, Cryptic Rite and Chivalric Orders of Knighthood. It is this latter branch that smacks of Templarism, containing the Chivalric distinctions of; Knight of the Red Cross, Knight of Malta, and Knight of the Temple (Knight Templar). These Chivalric Masons meet in preceptories or commandries generally named after heroes of the Crusades, for example, "King Baldwin Preceptory." The Templarism does not end here for modern Freemasonry, as even its group for young men is called De Molay after the martyr of the Knights Templar whom this organization chose as its namesake. They believe De Molay to represent the ultimate in bravery. It has been said that the York Rite of Masonry carries its link to Templarism openly, while the Scottish Rite carries its Templarism a little closer to the vest.

If we assert, as we must do, that Freemasonry is originally a Scottish peculiarity, we must, of course, bastion our belief with proof and this proof starts with the Masonic guilds. Guilds of masons had existed since early Medieval times not only in Scotland, but all over Europe. These fraternities were something of a mixture of a trade organization and a trade union, bent on protecting the interests of those participating in a particular trade. The art of cutting stone, and erecting it to make fine buildings, was of particular importance from earliest times, and so it is likely that masons were one of the first trades that sought to protect their own interests in every way possible. However most modern Freemasons have probably never come any closer to real masonry than the erection of a small garden wall and the Craft admits itself to be 'speculative', in other words, although it often uses the garbled terminology of the old mason's skills, it does not seek to sell the labor of its members as builders into the market place and could not provide those skills even if it did. Rather the symbols of the operative Mason are used by the speculative Masons, or Freemasons as they are more commonly known, to draw parallels to man's daily morality and inevitable mortality.

The stonemasons guilds existed everywhere, but it was in Scotland that real, horny handed, denizens of the chisel and the mallet first gave way to speculative Freemasonry. This is a very complicated subject, and the import of events in Scotland have formed the corpus of great books on the subject. For the sake of brevity we will restrict ourselves to certain 'known' events and then allow our reader to be the judge of these matters. The first evidence is based upon a tradition, so it cannot be considered entirely reliable, but since it fits into a continuum that is provable it is worth mentioning that as early as 1441 James II, who was King of Scotland at the time, appointed the St. Clair (Sinclair) family as Patrons and protectors of Scottish Masons. The King made this a hereditary office and declared that annual meetings would be held in Killwinning, Scotland.

This early date roughly coincides with the building of Rosslyn Chapel, near Edinburgh, and it is upon the bastion of this sturdy little Gothic masterpiece that so many claims for the origin of speculative Freemasonry rest.

Rosslyn Chapel was built by William Sinclair. It was commenced in 1446 and took about 40 years to complete. The word 'complete' in this context could be rather misleading, for it is still often claimed that what presently stands at Rosslyn is only the 'Lady Chapel' of what was eventually intended to be a large collegiate Church. It is assumed that the Sinclair family ran out of money to take the project any further, and so, even today, Rosslyn Chapel stands incomplete. We have studied these assertions, both through research and on site, and it is our contention, a belief that we share in common with many observers, that Rosslyn was never intended to be anything more than it is today and that even to call it 'a church or chapel' is misleading.

The authors Christopher Knight and Robert Lomas probably came closest to the mark in their excellent book, 'The Hiram Key', in suggesting that Rosslyn Chapel is intended to be a Medieval reconstruction of part of Solomon's Temple, which once stood in Jerusalem. If this assumption is correct, it answers many questions immediately. For a start we could not be surprised that the family who chose to grace Scotland with this admittedly 'European' version of what had originally been a truly 'Eastern' building was that of the Sinclairs. The reader will recall that one of the very first families to stand out as noteworthy in the history of Templarism was that of St. Clair, which gave land in Scotland for the building of the first Templar establishment outside of France and the Holy Land. As we saw earlier, it has been suggested that, Hughes de Payens, first Grand Master of the Templar Order, had been or still was, married to a St. Clair heiress. There is no doubting that the St. Clairs are of French origin, or that St. Clair, eventually became Sinclair.

The greatest aspiration of the Templars was towards that very edifice after which the whole Templar order was named, for they were, "The Poor Knights of Christ and the Temple of Solomon." It was in this location that the Templars found their first accommodation, and tradition has it that they dug extensively on the site, looking for something of value.

Of all the lands of Europe available, only a century or so after the whole Templar order had been made illegal, only Scotland offered the right family, sufficient funds, and a free enough political system to consider replicating something in stone that quite clearly represented a structure that went to the very heart of Templar beliefs and veneration.

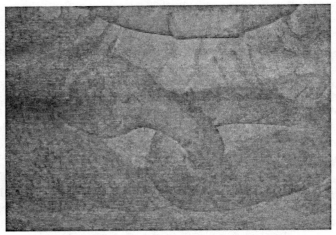

Serpents at base of Apprentice Pillar,
Rosslyn Chapel

Rosslyn Chapel is the most breathtaking exercise in stone carving that we have ever seen. From end to end and from floor to ceiling, there is barely a square foot of exposed stone that isn't ornamented in some way. The rich confection of styles and subject matter takes on the proportions of a 'Gothic dream', in which characters from the Old Testament, common workers from the 15th century, and nature gods of unknown ancestry vie for predominance amidst an endless tracery of leaves, stems and flowers. In proportion,

Rosslyn is said to be an exact replica of that sacred Temple built by Solomon. The two ornate pillars are said to be representations of the two great pillars that adorned the entrance to the Temple. It is the apprentice pillar that draws perhaps a subtle link to the actual building of the Temple. At the base of the apprentice pillar, eight serpents are entwined around the base forming an approximate octagonal shape, a staple of Templar architecture. It is our belief, and we must confess we are not the first to stumble on this, that the serpents represent the Shamir used by Solomon to carve the Temples stones. According to legend, King Solomon was commanded by God to build his temple without the aid of metal tools. Solomon is said to have employed the beast known as the "Shamir", which was a serpent like creature with the magical ability to carve rock with its slithering body.

In totality Rosslyn Chapel is extraordinary, and so far above hyperbole that, after visiting the site, and then finding oneself standing again in the clear Scottish air, words are entirely meaningless in terms of the overall experience.

In all probability what matters most about Rosslyn Chapel is the fact that it was created by a family which had enjoyed Templar sympathies from the very start, and which had maintained those leanings throughout the whole period of Templar existence. Surely, if we could prove that this same family had been present in Freemasonry since its inception, and we could also show that, from the start, Freemasonry allied itself with Templarism, and in the very area where Rosslyn stands, then the connection is proven. If the tradition relating to the granting of the protection of masons to the Sinclair family by James II is simply that - a tradition, then it is one that is likely to be based on solid foundations all the same. And it is another tradition that asserts William Sinclair, the builder of Rosslyn Chapel, was the man responsible for forming his masons into this organization.

The earliest Scottish reference to a 'speculative' Lodge of Freemasons comes from a later date, in fact a charter of 1598, though this is still well over a century before Grand Lodge in London was formed. The first speculative lodge was already known in the 1598 charter as 'The Old St. Mary's Lodge', which in itself ought to tell us that it was not, at that time, a new innovation. It was located in Edinburgh, which is only a few miles from Roslin and for some time after this successive charters, signed by Scottish monarchs, attest to the fact that the Sinclair family had historical rights to Scottish Freemasonry which predominated over those of other families.

No matter how much other writers hedge around the fact, this is the sum total of information that 'could' connect the St. Clairs and Sinclairs of Templarism, with the same family and Freemasonry. In other words there is not, and probably never will be, any absolute, written proof that there is a definite connection between Templarism and early Scottish speculative Freemasonry.

As researchers of long standing we have to observe that, even in the absence of actual proof of a particular fact, there are times when the law of probabilities comes into play to such an extent that the weight of circumstantial evidence must be taken into account. We believe this to be the case with regard to the Templar - Masonic connection and we suggest that the story of the merging of one into the other is probably as follows.

Alan's own previous research has shown conclusively that there are aspects of Rosslyn Chapel, both in terms of its Gothic construction, and its specific location, that would have led its builders to be very careful about revealing evidence of the secrets it contains. For example, the distance between Rosslyn Chapel and the Temple of Solomon, which it is purported to replicate, as a 'Great Circle' distance is exactly 1/10th of the circumference of the Earth. Taken with all Alan's other evidence that locks together the Gothic builders with very much older traditions of geometry and mathematics, we do not believe this astounding fact to have been a coincidence. We also believe, again primarily as a result of Alan's previous discoveries, that the very nature of Gothic architecture contains aspects of geometry that were not yet in the public domain at the time Rosslyn Chapel was constructed. Alan has shown in 'The Rose and the Grail' that these were matters well understood by the Templars, and this belief can be substantiated by a study of numerous examples of Templar and Cistercian buildings from the period when the Templars reigned supreme.

In other words, Rosslyn Chapel is replete with significant signposts that were also relevant to Templar and Cistercian efforts in architecture and is entirely consistent with structures of a date that predates Rosslyn Chapel by at least three centuries.

Bearing these facts in mind we suggest that William

Sinclair, the builder of Rosslyn Chapel, understood very well that at least a proportion of the masons constructing the edifice would find themselves party to mathematical and geometric secrets that he would not have wished to pass into the public domain. As a result he tied these masons together into the tightest of guilds, replete with horrible oaths of retribution handed out to anyone who betrayed the trust of the new fraternity. In all probability he offered these men, in return, a promise of work in Scotland for the remainder of their careers.

Logically the sons of many of these original workers would have become masons and stone carvers themselves, and they may have participated in the construction of Rosslyn Chapel, the building of which spanned more than one generation. It is the belief of other researchers, and ourselves, that the original 'guild' formed by William Sinclair, did not cease to govern a certain percentage of Scottish masons, even once Rosslyn Chapel was completed. Gradually members of these original families would have found work in the district other than that geared towards matters architectural. But these men were bound together by blood oaths that endured for generations, since there had undoubtedly been advantages of preference, welfare and mutual aid written into the original concept of the pledge made to William Sinclair. Quite naturally, William had based his proto-Masonic guild on the workers who had once created Solomon's Temple, of which Rosslyn was a partial copy. These matters conferred a 'special status' on the workers involved, and one that their sons and grandsons did not wish to relinquish.

By the 15th or 16th century the original conception of a 'special fraternity' endured, though it was obvious that not everyone seeking admittance, or inheriting a family association, was involved in building, and so what had been an 'operative guild' became a 'speculative lodge'. Exactly when this took place is not known, but the charter of 1598 infers that it happened at some time prior to that date. We respectfully submit that the aforementioned Killwinning Lodge had originally staked its claim based on manuscripts dated to 1670, but the Halliwell manuscript predates it by 280 years.

From its very inception Freemasonry, in its many and varied forms, has associated itself with Templarism, though to do so openly before the 18th century might have been very dangerous. The Templars were, by their very nature, a secret fraternity, and we have little idea of the rituals or practices that went on behind closed Templar doors. It would therefore be impossible to know how many present Masonic rituals might owe their origins to similar practices undertaken by Templars. But the same may not be true in reverse. Encapsulated into the Royal Arch Ritual of modern Freemasonry is what appears to be a blow by blow account of certain discoveries that may have been made by those first Templar Knights who labored for so long in the environs of Solomon's Temple in Jerusalem early in the 12th century. As far as we can ascertain this component of Masonic ritual has been present since the inception of Freemasonry. The very part of Solomon's Temple described in this passage is synonymous with that replicated in the very design and fabric of Rosslyn Chapel.

Of course much of modern Freemasonry claims to derive its origins from uniquely 'English' sources and this is particularly true with regard to York Rite Freemasonry. Some members of this fraternity, now distributed throughout the world and especially well represented in the Americas, may deny any connection with Scottish Rite, which carried the 'Sinclair' badge for so many centuries. The Chivalric degrees of York Rite Freemasonry are unique amongst its counterparts in that they are based exclusively on Christianity, whilst all other branches of the Craft only require from their members an admittance of a belief in a supreme deity. In this sense, save for the Chivalric order of Knight Templar, one need not be a professed Christian to join the ranks of Masonry's various branches.

Nevertheless York Rite Freemasonry, by its own admission, also contains supposed aspects of Templarism, and if we could show that, it too, ultimately owed its existence to Scotland, it would become more likely that all Templar associations with Freemasonry stemmed from that country.

Nobody disputes that a Masonic Lodge existed in the city of York prior to the foundation of English Grand Lodge in 1717, though for how long this Lodge has prospered is not known. But this Lodge, existent before the tenets of English Freemasonry were drawn together in London, is undoubtedly the home of York Rite Freemasonry. This was a period when many people were leaving England, to make a home for themselves in many different parts of the world and the fact that York Rite Freemasonry is so well represented in the United States and in Canada bears testimony to the fact that it was taken there before Grand Lodge absorbed York into its own brand of the Craft.

York Rite Freemasonry claims for itself a pedigree reaching back into Anglo Saxon England, and the reign of the first English King, Athelstan. who reigned from 925 to 939. Athelstan was the grandson of the more famous Alfred the Great and his chief claim to fame was that he conquered Northumberland, and also invaded Scotland, inflicting a crushing blow in the northern kingdom.

To understand how York Rite Freemasonry may have developed it is important to discover what was happening on the English throne at the start of the 18th century. The Restoration of the monarchy, after the English Civil War of the 17th century, had brought an uneasy truce between the Stuart Kings of England and their subjects, but not for long. Although Charles II ruled with some success, he did not have a legitimate heir, and so the crown passed to his younger brother James. Although of a moderate and ecumenical bent, James II was an avowed Catholic and that was enough to ensure that he would be hated by a large faction of powerful Protestants in England. He was unceremoniously thrown out of England, and the crown of England, Scotland, Wales and Ireland was offered to his sister Mary, and her Protestant Dutch husband, William of Orange in 1689. Mary died quite quickly, and when William of Orange also died in 1702, James' daughter Anne became Queen. These rulers were all nominally 'Stuart' but they were also Protestants. In any case they were stopgap rulers, for with the death of Queen Anne in 1714 the Elector of Hanover, George, was crowned King of England, Scotland Wales and Ireland. With his accession the crown passed out of the hands of the Stuart dynasty for good, however it would not be deemed dead in the eyes of some Freemasons. It is said by some that the Master Mason degree of Freemasonry was altered to include covert Stuart symbolism. These symbols included the Temple being an allegory for the Stuart monarchy, the murder of the Master of the Temple, Hiram, was an allusion to the beheading of Charles I. Additionally, to the Jacobites, the name given to the followers of King James, Queen Henrietta was referred to as the widow. By mere familial connection, this would make her son James II, the widows son, which is a term of Masonic significance. So some would say there can be no arguing the fact that at one point Freemasonry had a strong infiltration of Jacobite sentiments.

It is absolutely no coincidence that English Freemasonry

was born only three short years after the Hanoverian accession mentioned earlier. Up to that time Freemasonry did exist, even in London, but since it was so often seen as having an essentially Scottish origin, and was allied to the Stuart cause, its open practice would have been dangerous in such a heady political and religious period. The form of Freemasonry accepted by Grand Lodge was a synthesized form, entirely acceptable to the German born monarch, whose own family members soon became English Masons. Under the peculiar circumstances of the 'dynastic hinterland' at the end of the 17th century, it is easy to see how York Rite Freemasonry came about.

The region which today we know as the Netherlands, or Holland, gave rise to a group of people who are known in English speaking circles as 'The Dutch'. This term indicates that the people of the region were synonymous, at least in the English mind, with German speaking peoples, the early representatives of which had been the Anglo-Saxon rulers of England. The first of these rulers to effectively quash the Scots had been Athelstan, who was also revered in the York area for his advances in Church architecture, and simply because he was the first true King of all England.

The Protestant power base of 17th and 18th century England could justify the Dutch, and then ultimately the German, connection with the British crown on the grounds that our first, and most cohesive monarchs had also been German. It was therefore understandable that a king such as Athelstan should find favor at this time. It is our contention that York Rite Freemasonry, with its peculiarly 'English' overtones was probably the invention of one family - the Howards.

The Howards had been tremendously powerful in England for centuries, having been, since the days of Richard III, the Dukes of Norfolk. However, one branch of the family, headed by a noted turncoat and political opportunist by the name of Charles, ultimately became Dukes of Carlisle, which is in North West England, very close to the Scottish border. There they intermarried with the D'acre and Greystoke families, gaining vast estates in Yorkshire, to add to those in Cumberland.

The Third Earl of Carlisle, another Charles, fell out with his political contemporaries in the North West, and decided to build himself a fantastic new seat, close to York, in Yorkshire. This house,

Castle Howard, was built on the ruined foundations of an Anglo Saxon castle called Henderskelf. The House was commenced in about 1700, while Queen Anne was still on the throne of England. Nobody can say if Charles Howard, Third Earl of Carlisle was an early Freemason, but he had all the right credentials, not least of all a protracted period of family history on the Scottish borders, where Scottish Rite Freemasonry was already rife. However, Castle Howard positively shouts Freemasonry, from the pyramids and the obelisk in the grounds, to the Bacchanite, Cerenite and astronomical treatment of the Grand Hall, staircase and dome. And there is little doubt that this branch of the Howard family have been staunch Freemasons up to the present day. In fact, even before this section of the Howard family split from its Norfolk counterparts, it is known that the Dukes of Norfolk were early Freemasons.

The Third Earl of Carlisle knew where his bread was buttered in London, and he had held positions of responsibility and power under Queen Anne. What is more, unlike the Dukes of Norfolk, who had always been avowed Catholics, the Howard Dukes of Carlisle were Protestant by inclination. It is therefore highly likely that Charles, though a keen Mason, would have wished to distance himself from Scottish Rite Freemasonry, many of the members of which were plotting the return of the Stuart monarchs. As a result it seems highly likely that Charles Howard was instrumental in either taking Freemasonry in York and molding it to his own inclination, or else created it from scratch. He replaced the Stuart affiliation with one based on early Anglo Saxon history, which showed England as superior to the Scots and he avowed Christianity to lie at the center of the York Rite, which was not the case with Scottish Rite Freemasonry.

Ultimately it is likely that aspects of York Rite Freemasonry did find their way into the synthesis of Masonic beliefs that were adopted by Grand Lodge in 1717, as were many other skeins of Masonic thought. But by this time the York Rite had gained a credence of its own, which it continued to enjoy, not least of all in the isolation of outposts of the Empire, where it flourished, far from the guiding hand of Grand Lodge.

Replete though it is with Christian symbolism, York Rite Freemasonry still espouses Templar beliefs - probably to a greater extent than any other branch of Freemasonry, and in this regard it is representative of the Sinclair's earlier, Scottish Rite Freemasonry.

We are fully aware that this interpretation of the origins of York Rite Freemasonry will not be to everyone's taste, though we do feel it to be more historically credible than the mishmash of half truths that lie at its core as explained by supposed historians of the fraternity. Many of these people have not been especially familiar with the realities of early English history, and fail to understand the nature of the Kingdom in Anglo Saxon times. The association of York Rite Freemasonry with King Athelstan served many useful purposes to Charles Howard and his contemporaries and, failing the return of the Stuarts after 1700, it could hardly fall foul of an England run by either Dutch or German Monarchs.

The reader will either accept or reject our account of how York Rite Freemasonry came about. We have shown that Templarism has been endemic to Freemasonry from its very inception, long before the formation of Grand Lodge in London. It is apparent that the transformation from Templarism to Freemasonry took place in Scotland at the time of the building, by the Templar family Sinclair, of Rosslyn Chapel. From that point it grew from an 'operative guild', to a 'speculative Lodge system'. During the reign of James I, a Scottish born Stuart King, it traveled from Scotland with the King and his ministers, and took root in England. Ultimately it fell into disfavor during the difficulties experienced by the Stuart Monarchs, and lived underground until the Hanoverian accession. At this time it was 'massaged' to accommodate the needs of the moment and its Stuart sympathies were exorcised. York Rite Freemasonry was a 'halfway station in this process'. Too lacking in Stuart sympathies for the Scottish taste, and yet not peculiarly to the liking of the ruling classes in the South of England.

From first to last, and despite the patently absurd assurances to the contrary by representatives of Grand Lodge London, Freemasonry, no matter what baggage it had gained on the way, is Templarism reborn, at a time when to be a Templar in a Christian country, would have meant certain death. Not only does this fact give credence to its avowed secrecy but the 'closed' nature of its evolving rituals allowed many of them to become virtual 'time capsules' of Templar thought. It is hard to imagine how any reasonable student of these matters could now fail to accept Freemasonry as a legitimate branch of Templar survival.

Despite recent setbacks in England, Freemasonry is flourishing still. In a recent Time Magazine article, it was reported that membership in the world's oldest fraternal organization is on the rise. It is a rich and powerful institution, based on an acceptance of the tenets of enterprise and Capitalism entirely consistent with what we know of Templarism. Like the Templars, Freemasons in general advocate a policy of 'tolerance in religion' and most of the differing branches of Freemasonry are willing to accept members of any religion and denomination so long as they profess a belief in a monotheistic faith. This would include Catholics, contrary to popular belief. An interesting insight becomes obvious when the reverse issue is addressed however, because it is still a crime against the Catholic Church, punishable by excommunication, for a practicing Catholic to also belong to a Masonic institution. It might be suggested that the Catholic Church has retained a virtual paranoia concerning matters Masonic, and this in itself may be very telling. The Church has been, and still is, very much aware that it was complicit in the destruction of the Templars. This is a historical fact, and one that the Church cannot alter, even if it may have regretted its own actions subsequently. We cannot find a single instance of any Masonic group openly seeking to treat the Catholic Church with the same disdain which the Craft has received time and again from Rome, and yet the Catholic Church, even in these enlightened days, will not allow Masonic membership for its adherents.

We would suggest that the reasoning behind Rome's attitude towards Freemasonry is entirely consistent with its certain knowledge that there is a direct connection between Templarism and Freemasonry. It is also likely that the Vatican finds it difficult to accept that the remnants of an institution it once betrayed so completely are not bent on revenge. Present in every country in the free world the Catholic authorities see, at least in their own perception, a red cross on every Masonic breast. It is difficult to enjoy the fruits of such a hollow victory as that of 1307 when such a tangible and even powerful specter is constantly present at the feast.

Chapter Ten

The Templar Homeland?

Like any major international company, which is essentially
what the Templar Order had become by 1307, the
organization had branches everywhere. It is precisely in
recognition of this fact, which has been so often overlooked, that we
both became convinced that the Knights Templar could never have
been totally destroyed by the actions of one European monarch, even
though that king had the backing of a tame Pope. We hope that we
have shown conclusively in the preceding chapters that the Templars
did survive, and in a multitude of different ways. All the same, we
were aware that, in the years following the loss of the Holy Land, the
Templars had shown a continuing desire to create a 'state' of their
own. Undoubtedly this was part of the reason for the attack made
upon the Templars by Philip Le Bel of France, since it must have
seemed most likely to him that Southern France was the area that the
Templars coveted the most. The Templars were strong in this area,
with foundations all over the Languedoc and their influence extended
into the Camarge and in the foothills of the Pyres. But as more and
more information came to hand, and our own previous researches
threw up crumbs of evidence from this source or that, we gradually
became aware that the whole issue regarding the South of France
may have been yet another smoke screen, deliberately created by the
Templars themselves to prevent interference in their genuine plans
for nationhood.

These crumbs of evidence eventually became a veritable
banquet and we are now left in no doubt that the Templars did indeed
manage, against all odds, to carve out their own nation. It wasn't
some Eldorado in the New World, nor a hidden kingdom of the
Prester John variety in darkest Africa. In fact the Templars remained
absolutely central to everything that was happening in Europe, and
what is more they were partly instrumental in the formation of the
Western World as we know it today. The Templar State was, and is,

Switzerland.

So obvious is this assertion, and so overwhelming is the evidence to support it, that we both remain astounded that it does not stand as common knowledge. We hope to put this right, and though our previous chapters show just how widespread was the Templar organization, and in how many different forms it survived, we remain absolutely convinced that it is to Switzerland that we should predominantly look for the survival of Templarism.

On the eve of that fateful day in 1307 nothing like the present State of Switzerland even existed. The whole area of the Alps comprised a complex series of nominally independent dukedoms and fiefs, most of which had come to fall under the sway of the Holy Roman Empire. German influence was also strong in the area. At the end of the 13th century, three of these little regions, Uri, Schwyz and Unterwalden took the first tentative steps towards autonomy, and by so doing showed where Templar influence was growing strongly. It was in the year 1291 that Uri, Schwyz and Unterwalden signed a solemn compact of mutual assistance. And it is from about this time that folk tales began to spread regarding the assistance that the new compact received from white clad knights, whose vestments bore the familiar red cross of the Templars. In fact it would seem, as we will look at in due course, that these folk tales, found their way into the legend of the Swiss flag. The little regions fought ferociously, both against the Holy Roman Empire, and against the German domination that had always been so strong in the area. Very soon they were joined by Zurich, Glarus, Bern, Lucerne and Zug, forming an alliance that began to resist foreign domination in an effective way. Swiss soldiers became legendary in Europe for their tenacity and bravery, a reputation of which the Swiss, though now fiercely neutral, are understandably proud.

It took time to weld the Cantons, as they became known, into a truly cohesive political and economic force, but as far as foreign domination was concerned, the battle was effectively over by 1499, when the cooperating regions were granted virtual autonomy. This region of Europe would certainly not have been a mystery to the Templar knights, even prior to 1307. The movement of soldiers, and goods, back and forth between Southern France and Northern Italy, demanded the use of one or other of the mountain passes which are now part of Swiss territory. Many authors have shown the very strong association between Templar history and ideals, and a particular French dynasty - the Merovingians. Clovis I, the first Christian French monarch had been born of this bloodline, though it had fallen in the 8th century with the murder of Dagobert II and the installation of a new ruling elite. However, it is almost certain that Merovingians, and what they had represented, lay at the heart of the Templarism and the Merovingians had been especially strong in the area we today call Switzerland. Chief amongst their strongholds in the Alps had been the town which today is known as Sion, the very name of which shouts Templarism, and lives as a testimony to the virtual obsession regarding Sion - Jerusalem, that lay at the heart of the First Crusade.

The Merovingians had kept their chief mint at Sion, and the place was still somewhat important in the Middle Ages. The Templars will have known it well. As to their actual holdings in the area prior to 1307, the evidence is somewhat blurred, but it is known that there was, eventually, a significant presence of Knights Hospitaller in the region. Since most Templar property was, by Papal ruling, passed to the much smaller Hospitalers after 1307, it is highly likely that the Swiss holdings had originally been Templar ones.

To really examine this whole possibility we must travel back to a period prior to 1307. The fall of Acre, and the loss of the last toe hold of Christianity in the Levant made the intended destruction of the Templars that much easier for Philip Le Bel. The Order's reputation had reached an all time low and it must have seemed to many, and especially to the crowned heads of Europe, that the whole institution had become a dangerous anachronism. But to assume that the Templars themselves remained blissfully unaware of the way the wind was blowing is surely to be naive. And the fact that tales of white clad knights assisting the first struggling Swiss Cantons, preceded the events of 1307 surely adds weight to the notion that the Templars began to take steps to ensure their own survival, as soon as Acre had fallen, in 1291. In fact Acre fell in May, 1291, and the compact signed between the first three Cantons, Uri, Schwyz and Unterwalden, was signed in August of 1291. Taken in context with all our other observations, we see the two events as being closely related.

So, at the self and same moment in history when the Templar Order found itself facing public approbation, and when the crowned heads of Europe at last seemed powerful enough to stem its influence, a new and remote mountain state, though one on the very frontiers of France, began to forge its independence, with the use of a soldiery that became synonymous with efficiency, bravery and ferocity.

We have always believed that the search for a single treasury of Templar gold was something of a red herring, and we hope that we have shown adequately that such a notion was a 'medieval concept'. Kings and great men of the period had always kept such treasuries, and so it was natural for them to assume that the Templars behaved in a similar manner. But the Templar way was more modern because the vast majority of the wealth owned by the institution was being put to good use all of the time. However, there must have been depositories in many parts of France, together with valuable possessions that the Templars wished to retain. It is our firm belief that though Jacques de Molay, and many other Templars were put to death in the years following 1307, Philip Le Bel was, nevertheless, out maneuvered by the Order as a whole with regard to such treasure, and that the removal of the Templar valuables from France probably commenced some years before he directly attacked the institution.

We have seen that trade routes to Northern Italy ran through the passes of Switzerland, and these must have been paths regularly trodden by Templar traders. It would have been simplicity itself to arrange for Templar gold to be transferred to predetermined 'safe' sites in the mountains, without ever raising the slightest suspicion in Paris. The evidence shows that Philip Le Bel kept a close eye on the Templar fleet, based on the West coast of France in La Rochelle. His efforts were, in any case, to no avail, for history relates that the fleet disappeared on or about October 12th, just a day or so before Philip's net closed around the Order. It is therefore perhaps understandable for historians to have assumed that all the Templar wealth from France was aboard the fleet, but we are of the opinion that this was not at all the case. It would have been monumental incompetence for the Templar Order to put all its eggs in one basket, and particularly a basket that stood so firmly within French territory. In all probability while Philip's attention was deliberately being focused on the West coast of France, anything of value that the Templars wished to preserve was being slowly, and systematically transferred overland to the East. There were dozens of routes from France into the Alps, many of them running through the remotest parts of Philip's territory. Besides this consideration it should be remembered that Philip Le Bel intended his actions to be kept secret until the very last minute, so although his forces may have been 'observing' what must have appeared to be normal Templar activities on the trade routes, there is absolutely no evidence that they were 'examined' in any way. And if all, or some of this, appears to be circumstantial, the greatest proof for our assertions lies in what Switzerland eventually became.

Even the present Swiss economy is based on banking, farming, pharmaceuticals, and high precision engineering. None of these economically crucial components of Switzerland's ultimate rise to success are at all out of kilter with what is known of Templar Inc., at the time of the 1307 attacks. The Templars were already the leading bankers of the world and with vast estates all over the known world they were highly efficient and very capable farmers. Their involvement in alchemy and the foundations of modern chemistry could easily have laid the foundation for an eventual excursion into pharmaceuticals, and the necessities of warfare, navigation and architecture had made them the engineers par excellence of their day. We were stunned by the nature of some of the flags, not only of the Swiss Cantons, but of the regions within the Cantons. We reproduce some of them in the appendix at the end of the book and we would wish to draw the readers attention to the proliferation of Templar crosses contained within their construction.

One flag in particular, that of Zurich Hongg, leaves us almost speechless. It contains not only the Templar Cross, but also a representation of a vine and a pruning knife. The whole concept of 'Viticulture', lies so close to the heart of the assertion that the bloodline of the Merovingian kings survived after the death of Dagobert II that, once again, we fail to understand why nobody has recognized the significance previously. Readers interested in this aspect of the bloodlines' regularly associated with the so called Prieure de Sion, as an adjunct to Templarism, might care to read 'The Holy Blood and the Holy Grail, by Baigent, Leigh and Lincoln, where the whole matter is discussed at great length.

It is no coincidence, we believe, that the very flag of Swiss nationhood is simply a reversed version of the most famous Templar motif, for instead of being a red cross on a white field, it is a white cross on a red field. Our research into the origins of the Swiss flag, revealed what would seem to link the folk tales of white clad knights fighting bloody battles for the fledgling confederation. It should be noted here that the Swiss flag takes its design from that of the canton of Schwyz which was one of the founding members of the union and from which the country takes its name. However, the flag was in use by the canton of Schwyz prior to the confederation of 1291. The Flag unlike that of other countries is not rectangular, but rather is perfectly square. We cannot help but draw the immediate Templar and Masonic significance of this shape. The story of the Swiss flag goes that the red symbolizes blood while the cross the obvious religious connection.

According to the legends and folk tales of this forest canton, the Schwyz soldiers, while battling in the Southern Alps, suffered numerous losses. So great was the blood shed, that the white tunics of the soldiers were stained completely with blood leaving the only unblemished spot in the shape of the Holy cross that they wore over their left breast. That same cross appears in the upper right corner of the Schwyz flag. If one were to take a garment with a crest on the left breast and hold it up for someone to look at, that person would see the crest on their right hand side. We respectfully submit that the very flag of this neutral nation Switzerland, is none other than a representation of the garments worn by those Templars who fought for the freedom of the embryonic Swiss nation.

Switzerland remains unique amongst the nations of the world in a number of different ways. For one thing it never even became a true, federal state until the 19th century. Even today the Cantons, or regions, retain an incredible degree of autonomy. The people of the Cantons remain part of the greater Switzerland, not because they must, but simply because they wish, as free and independent Europeans, to do so. It is no secret that the modern State of Switzerland owes its great wealth predominantly to banking, and yet secrets there are in abundance. No modern world state is so closed to scrutiny, for the Swiss jealously guard their banking transactions in the name of 'confidentiality'; this to such an extent that it is absolutely impossible to assess just how rich the country really is. And since wealth is power, it is equally impossible to assess the impact that Swiss ideas may have had upon the modern world. A providential loan here, a refusal to support a regime there - and the implications for the world as a whole can be pivotal!

We are all aware of the present controversy regarding Switzerland's neutral stance in the Second World War, and the millions of dollars worth of German money that found its way into the State, much of it stolen from Jewish citizens of Europe. The truth may never be known, but the Swiss are so absolutely determined to keep their banking secrets, that they have been willing to pay out huge sums in reparation - even where no crime has actually been proven against them in the law courts of the world. But if Switzerland has been closed to the gaze of the globe in some ways, in others it has shone out as a bright star of tolerance, cooperation and free speech. It was more or less a foregone conclusion that the Savoy state of Geneva would eventually join the Swiss confederacy, and eventually this happened. And it is Geneva that was to become the center of a 'world awareness'. It was in Geneva that 'The League of Nations' was formed after the First World War, and it was also from Geneva that the International Red Cross sprang in the 19th century. We remind the reader that the emblem of the red cross is precisely that most revered by the Templars - a red cross on a white field.

Earlier still Switzerland had fostered the embryonic notion of Protestantism, which without the important bastion it found in Geneva, may never have survived to challenge the retarding and corrupt influences of the all-powerful Catholic Church in the 16th and 17th centuries. Despite many internal difficulties on the way Geneva, and Switzerland as a whole, became synonymous with the 'right to personally held beliefs.' In fact it is doubtful that Switzerland could have survived without this deeply held conviction. The country is a total anachronism, comprised of many different forms of Christianity, four different languages and a wealth of alternating traditions. Yet despite the many reasons for civil unrest Switzerland remains almost pathological in its quest for neutrality and has the reputation, deserved or not, of being perhaps the most 'conservative' and even the most 'boring' European State. Switzerland was at the very heart of the formation of the European Common Market, retaining a 'world consciousness' that belies its mountainous landscape. We would suggest that in every known way Switzerland represents exactly what a Templar state would have been destined to become and we would go so far as to suggest that if 'The Holy Grail' or the 'Ark of the Covenant' truly did exist in the modern world, the most likely place to find either of them would be in the dark recesses of some bank vault in Zurich or Geneva.

The tap roots of Swiss influence extend so deeply into the very foundations of the modern world that it would be impossible to ascertain where the furthest of them emerge. In a more local sense, some of those who have made it their life's work to understand the complexities of French history, even up to and including the 19th and 20th centuries have been aware of a strong but subversive Johannite thread running through the fabric of the French State. These influences helped to destroy Louis XVI and assisted in bringing revolutionary fervor to France. This little understood network of interrelating groups can be shown to have instigated occurrences, usually on French soil, that undermined the power and influence of the Catholic Church, that same institution that had turned so treacherously upon the Templars, one of its own Holy orders. And when the origin of such groups can be discovered, shadowy factions with Swiss connections inevitably have a part to play in the story. And what would be more natural for the true legatees of the Templar order, even after centuries, than to seek some degree of vengeance on the self and same agencies that sought to extinguish Templarism and all it had become - The French Crown and the Catholic Church?

The average Swiss citizen may know nothing whatsoever of the Templars, or indeed the true origins of their own state, but it is our heartfelt contention that underlying the whole Swiss experiment is the search for an equitable, democratic society, where each individual retains an importance to the whole, no matter what the language, political beliefs or religious persuasion of that person might be. The success or failure of such a system rests fairly and squarely on the caprices of human nature but we remain convinced that the best of what Switzerland represents conforms in great measure to the 'New Jerusalem' that was the earnest wish of people such as St. Bernard of Clairvaux, who did more to inspire the great enterprise of Templarism than any other man. What became impossible in the desert fastness of the Levant, just perhaps, was made manifest amidst the snowy peaks of the Swiss Alps.

It is highly likely that Jacques de Molay, maintaining his silence through years of captivity, before suffering the most horrible of deaths in Paris, knew that his institution was safe, buying that safety to an even greater degree with his silence, patience and, ultimately, his courage.

In the course of this book we have followed the white clad knights across the length and breadth of Europe, into the Mediterranean, and out beyond the Pillars of Hercules to Britain, and to the new lands beyond the setting sun. The skeletons of their great castles and ports stand gaunt against the dawn of many lands, and the virtual myth that they have become reverberates around the globe nearly seven hundred years after their supposed demise. But of all the suggested answers to the mystery of the disappearing Templars, together with their vast wealth, we hold fast to the belief that neither truly vanished at all. And the fact that it seems that nobody has realized the truth in such a long span of time merely bears testimony to the eternal truth that 'a mystery' is usually infinitely more intriguing than its solution.

Conclusions

Untangling The Web

Within the pages of this book we are both very aware that we have been walking in the footsteps of the giants of Templar research. To that end it is likely that some of our ideas will be seen as contentious. However, we have endeavored to look at the period of the Templar knights, not so much with the eyes of observers interested in myth, but rather as true historians would. As a result we are forced to conclude that the very nature of Templarism engendered a somewhat 'modern' feel for the way the world should be run, and particularly so in an economic sense. It is not our place to either accept or repudiate this economic model but it would be wrong to finish this book without making a few observations regarding our discoveries.

Nowhere, either in Europe or the known world, can we find an economic system such as that championed by the Templars that predates the order itself. Much has been written about the way the Renaissance, and the arrival of Protestantism, shook the Western World free from the restrictive hand of Medieval Catholicism, allowing knowledge to flourish, prompting scientific research and also promoting a form of Capitalism. We do not argue with these assertions, but rather would seek to inquire 'how' such things became possible. There are many possible answers, but it seems to us that the influence upon Europe of post-Templar thinkers such as Rene d'Anjou, may have had a great deal to do with the situation. A most influential monarch of the 15th century, Rene encouraged banking, showed an interest in knowledge other than that allowed by the Catholic Church, and was instrumental in influencing others to establish 'secular' centers of learning.

We would argue that this course of action is entirely in accord with what is known of the Templars, when all the hatred, propaganda and vitriol of those with the greatest interest in blackening the name of the order is removed. Conversely we would not wish to leave our readers with the impression that we in any way 'eulogize' the Templar order as a whole. Doubtless sections of the institution were corrupt, high handed and downright bullying in their treatment of kings and commoners alike. The Templars were certainly not gods, and it is a profound mistake on the part of some, even in the modern world, to paint them as such. All the same, taken dispassionately, and on balance, there seems little doubt that an order which had formerly kept its secrets to itself, together with its unique methods of doing business, was suddenly forced onto the offensive, and that its response was not so much to change itself, but ultimately to alter the world in which it existed. Whether this process was 'conscious' on the part of any single 'unit' or 'branch' of post 1307 Templarism, is open to debate. We live in a Capitalistic world, which, although somewhat shaky at the time we write these words, has outlived the once ferocious onslaught of communism and overthrown a number of vicious dictatorships. Perhaps we see these processes as natural, and certainly we accept the validity of 'now'. But how much different might that 'now' have been if Philip Le Bel of France had not looked with such avaricious eyes at the Templars? 'You pays your money and you takes your choice'. Love it or loath it, Capitalism exists, and although there are voices that argue the contrary, it survives, generally speaking, within a democratic framework. As to whether this could ever have been the case without the events of Friday October 13th, 1307 is a matter for conjecture.

Appendix

Flags of the Swiss Cantons

Flags Of The Founding Cantons

The Flag of the Canton of Schwyz, from which the Country took both its National flag and its name .

The flag of the Canton of Uri, one of the three founding forest Cantons

The Flag of the Canton of Unterwalden. The cross in the second key was later replaced to a similar design to the first key.

Various Canton Flags

Ardez   **Niederrohrdorf**

Zurich   Zurich   Zurich
Hongg   Schwamendingen   Albisrieden

Bibliography

Our Sources Revealed

Addison, C.G.. Knights Templars.
   New York: Masonic Publishing Co., 1874

Baigent, Michael, Richard Leigh and Henry Lincoln. Holy Blood
and The Holy Grail.
   London: Jonathan Cape Ltd., 1982

Baigent, Michael, Richard Leigh. The Temple and The Lodge.
   Great Britain: Corgi, 1988

Barber, Malcolm. The Trial of the Templars.
   New York: Cambridge University Press, 1978

Barber, Malcolm. The New Knighthood.
   New York: Cambridge University Press, 1994

Bede. Historia Ecclesiastica Gentis Anglorum.
   London: Oxford, 1996

Bonjour, E, H.S. Offler and G.R. Potter. A Short History of
Switzerland.
   Oxford: Clarendon Press., 1952

Brown. Stellar Theology and Masonic Astronomy.
   Publisher and date unknown

Burman, Edward. Supremely Abominable Crimes.
   Great Britain: Allison & Busby, 1994

Butler, Alan. The Bronze Age computer Disc.
    London: Foulsham, 1998

Dafoe, Stephen A. Unholy Worship.
    Ontario: Templar Books, 1998

Deanesly, Margaret M.A. A History of the Medieval Church 590-1500.
    London: Methuen & Co. Ltd., 1962

Ellis. The Men and Message of the Old Testament
    London: Litergical Press, 1963

Gardner, Lawrence. Bloodline of the Holy Grail.
    London: Element, 1996

Grant, Michael. Constantine The Great.
    New York: Charles Scribner's Sons, 1993

Howard, Michael. The Occult Conspiracy.
    Vermont: Destiny Books, 1989

Knight, Christopher, Robert Lomas. The Hiram Key
    London: Arrow Books, 1996

Knight, Christopher, Robert Lomas. The Second Messiah:
London: Century Books, 1997

Mackay, Albert. The History of Freemasonry
    New York: Gramercy, 1996

Picknett, Lynn. Clive Prince. The Templar Revelation
    New York: Bantam 1997

Pike, Albert. Morals and Dogma.
    Washington: The Roberts Publishing Co., 1871

Robinson, John J. Born in Blood: The Lost Secrets Of
Freemasonry.
New York: Evans, 1989

Rosslyn, Earl of. Rosslyn Chapel.
Rosslyn Chapel Trust, 1997

Seward, Desmond. The Monks Of War.
London: Penguin Books, 1972

Schultz. Movement and Rhythns of the Stars
New York: Floris, 1963

Visit Us On The World Wide Web

www.templarbooks.com

To Learn More About The Authors

www.templarbooks.com/butler-dafoe/